The Devil and Joe Daily

by

Tim D. Smith

Copyright @ Tim D. Smith, July 2014

ISBN 978-1-312-32770-2

Printed in the United States of America

Without limiting the rights under copyright reserved above, no part of this publication may be reproduced, stored in or introduced into a retrieval system, or transmitted, in any form, or by any means (electronics, mechanical, photocopying, recording, or otherwise) without the prior written permission of both the copyright owner and the above publisher of this book.

Note:

This is a work of fiction. Names, characters, places, and incidents either are the product of the author's imagination or are used fictitiously, and any resemblance to actual persons, living or dead, business establishments, events, or locales is entirely coincidental.

The scanning, uploading and distribution of this book via the Internet or via any other means without the permission of the publisher is illegal and punishable by law. Please purchase only authorized editions and do not participate or encourage piracy of copyrighted materials. Your support of the author's rights is appreciated.

Cover art designed by Hannah Hall.

This book is dedicated to her and her wonderful mother.

The Devil and Joe Daily

by Tim D. Smith

Chapter 1

If Joe Daily had known what was going to happen that night, he might not have gone to work.

He didn't mind going into the plant early on Sunday nights. Not anymore. There was a time when he had, but over the years he had submitted to the grind of work and grown accustomed to the realization that this was where he would labor until he retired. Maybe even until the end of his days. His younger dreams never involved working in a factory, and by no stretch of the imagination would he have pictured himself where he was today. In his younger days he always saw himself accomplishing grand things; he always thought his life would be somehow more meaningful. The last straw in his submission came three years ago when he lost Michelle. Now, he no longer minded going to the plant.

Joe's vacation during the Fourth of July shutdown had come and gone, and now August, which had only perched on the horizon briefly, had almost slipped by as well. The heat of middle Tennessee pervades and the manufacturing space of the main building, Plant 1, would be even hotter when all the presses began running. In fact, for the uninitiated the floor would seem unbearable. After all, the machines had to be hot enough to melt plastic, and with only fans pulling the air out the temperature inside rose all week until the weekend shutdown provided relief. During the week, Plastics International's work area was hot as hell.

Glenn, who is always the first of Joe's employees on Sunday night, arrived looking especially dapper because he had shaved, all but his moustache of course which hung from each corner of his mouth like a small vine. His faithful St. Louis Cardinals cap, soiled and stained with the remnants of two perfectly round marble-sized drops of dried plastic from when one of the presses erupted and burned the former boss Ross, sat atop his red hair. He carried a bulging Wal Mart plastic bag containing what Joe thought was probably Glenn's lunch.

"I got the two presses in the last bay," Glenn said. He grinned and his moustache rose and fell in an uneven way.

"That was nice of you." Joe flipped the switches on what was now the last press to begin heating.

"Fall football practice starts this week," Glenn said. Joe still needed to make out the duty roster, and Glenn often followed along as he did now. "Tennessee's gonna be good this year."

"Well, they usually are."

"What about your Commodores?"

"We need a quarterback. At least the one we have needs to do better. Anyway, we'll see how far they came in the offseason."

"You know, I don't give you as hard a time as everyone else. Why you keep pulling for that team?"

"I grew up here in Nashville, Glenn. Vandy has class. Now, I need to think and work on the list."

But now the only thing Joe could think about was the upcoming football season. Why *did* he keep pulling for Vanderbilt? Football in the south is a way of life, and Vandy was a longtime member of the Southeastern Conference, college football's version of the big leagues. The school's admission standards and rigorous academic offerings caused them to miss out on many blue chip recruits. Not too many players convinced of their chances at NFL careers wanted to spend thirty hours a week studying, not even for the assurance of skills and future job security.

By the time work at the plant had begun in full force and the presses were whirring, it seemed that Glenn had made certain every worker knew football was in the air. Even Old Man Moore, who was in a surprisingly good mood for a Sunday night, got in on the act. Several years earlier, a grinder cut off Moore's middle finger two joints down, and his favorite greeting was to yell "Hey!" and flip a bird, which was of course non-existent. Tonight though, he was giving everyone, including Joe, an index finger, a toothless smile, and a gruff "Number one, baby!"

By 4:30 with the presses running well, Joe was in no mood to even have supper in the break room. A fog of depression had settled over his countenance as clouds from the impending storm of football season approached. Carrying a Styrofoam cup of black coffee he dragged his fifty-year-old body out the back doors and slumped heavily on a seldom used wooden bench, the sounds of the machines fading replaced by the sound of the summer cicadas from the woods across the road behind the plant. Staring at the swirls of steam in the black liquid he wondered what life had in store for him as he fought a tidal wave of depression.

"Nice night for a stroll," a stranger standing in front of Joe said.

Joe, who had been deep in thought, jumped, startled, and the coffee sloshed onto his fingers and the ground.

"Jesus, I-"

"Is that taking the Lord's name in vain? I've always wondered," the man said smiling. Standing above Joe, the man seemed tall, accentuated by what appeared to be tailored slacks, a black short sleeve shirt that hugged his neck even without a collar, and a crop of stout salt and pepper hair that stood no more than a half- inch high on his head. His smile, sitting beneath his thin, dark moustache, would have been the envy of any movie star.

"I didn't notice you."

"Just out for an evening walk. Mind if I sit?"

"No. Not at all." Joe still hadn't recovered his wits enough to ask what the man was doing walking up to the back of the factory in the middle of the night to make conversation, but for some reason he wasn't suspicious of the stranger.

"You okay, friend?"

"It's Sunday night. To tell you the truth, I'm tired," Joe said, and that was the truth.

"Sunday. The Lord's day. I suppose one should tell the truth on a Sunday." He was smiling once more. "Of course, it's Monday by now."

"Of course."

"Then again, isn't every day the Lord's day?" The statement didn't sound or seem like a question, and it wasn't. The tall man continued. "If you could have anything you wanted in life," the man said and paused before continuing, "most anything, well let's just say anything, you know, to make the funk go away, what would it be?" He leaned back and stretched his long legs out straight. Joe noticed the man's slightly pointy, possibly Italian, boots with silver at the very end of the toes.

The first thing that popped to mind was Michelle, and rather than baring his soul to a complete stranger he rethought the question. The night had started so well, it seemed. Then Glenn had begun football talk. Every year at this time, it was football.

"Vandy would win the SEC," Joe said.

"Ah, Vanderbilt. They've broken some hearts over the years. Just the SEC? Why not win it all?"

"Sure. We'll have Vandy win it all," Joe said. His team. The Vanderbilt Commodores, perennial cellar dwellers in the conference. They had sure broken his heart his entire life.

"What would you give?"

Joe thought about Glenn's smirk. Sure, he was an innocent, good natured fan, but it sure would be nice to rub THAT in his face. Joe smiled.

"I'd give about anything," Joe said. "Name's Joe." He extended his hand and the stranger took it. Strong grip. Warm but dry. Something about that handshake, like a salesman, and Joe figured the man was a salesman. He had a strong intuition.

"My name is Appel. Allistair Appel."

The name had a nice ring to it.

"Nice to meet you, Mr. Appel."

"You can call me Al. Like the song."

"Okay, nice to meet you Al. So, you said you were out for a walk? What brings you up by here?"

"I hope I'm not intruding at the plant," Al said.

"No, it's okay. Right by the road and all. I'm surprised more people don't wander up, it's so close. It's my break time."

"I thought so," Al said. He looked to the sky and breathed deep, inhaling a long breath of fresh air. "So, you'd give anything for Vandy to win? Really win?"

Joe stared at the man. Speechless.

"Be careful what you wish for," Al said turning his attention fully on Joe. "You might just get it all."

The only thing Joe could do was laugh. This was Vandy they were talking about. And laugh Joe did, so hard he had to look down and rub the tears from his eyes. When he looked up once more, he was alone. Utterly alone.

Chapter 2

When nothing happened out of the ordinary during the next night's shift, Joe began to wonder if the tall man with the silver pointed shoes had even been real. Had Joe even met him? Was he losing his mind? If he was, he had every right. First of all, working midnights was not natural, and he was pretty sure that any number of studies had been done to support the claim. Human beings were meant to sleep at night.

Secondly, his stress level at work was bound to be taking some sort of toll on him. He had been supervisor of the entire shift now for almost four years, ever since Ross got burned and endured a long hospital stay and months of rehabilitation before retiring. Many said he got a settlement, and it wouldn't have surprised Joe one bit if that was fact. Being burned still wouldn't have made it worth it.

Then, there was Michelle. Any man would have been affected by that. Who couldn't be? If he was in the process of losing his mind, he had every right.

The conversation, or the dream if it hadn't been real, had him thinking though, and they weren't at all good thoughts. Joe had believed he was content, but he now realized that wasn't the case, far from it. It was the feeling he had early in his marriage to Michelle. Busy getting his degree in journalism and working, he had dreams of living in big cities and driving a nice car. The job in the plant paid the bills, though, and even after graduating and after all these years he remained. Why was he stuck here? Why did he stay here all these years and watch his life pass without so much as a whimper of resistance?

By the time he went home after the next shift, he busied himself with these very questions and even began to wonder if working at the plant was worthwhile anymore. He enjoyed it though, or at least he thought he did. It kept him occupied so he didn't think about things so much all the time. He had friends at the plant. They came to his house and watched football. They hung out sometimes on the weekends, and he watched them drink beer and took them home when they drank too much. But while all these things were worthwhile, Joe didn't really need to work anymore. There was the matter of the insurance after Michelle. The house was paid for, and what with his mundane and simple life he didn't need much. He didn't want much, or at least he hadn't thought he wanted much until recently. The thing he most wanted he couldn't have.

By the time Wednesday's shift rolled around, Joe had decided that Al was probably a dream, or at least a figment of an overactive imagination. During his first break, Glenn, who had filled all of the hoppers on the presses and given his breaks, joined him sipping coffee and sitting in front of the plant listening to the cycles of the machines and watching traffic trickle by in the night as people went about whatever business had them out so late.

"You ever see a guy walking around late at night?"

"You mean like a hobo or somethin'?" Glenn asked.

"No. I don't know. No, like any normal person, dressed nice?"

"I don't think so."

The topic of conversation sat there ready to die before Glenn rescued it.

"You see somebody?"

"No. Not really. No," Joe said. Then he continued. "I thought I saw a guy walking around back one night."

"Prowlin' around?"

"Just walking. Dressed nice. A tall guy wearing a black shirt. He had a thin moustache. Boots. He was out back."

"Never saw anybody out back," Glenn said.

"Well, if you see someone, would you come get me?"

"Sure. We'll check 'im out."

Joe and Glenn seemed to decide that would be a good course of action, and the conversation turned to sports. Of course. Glenn's Cardinals were making a run. By September they would be in first place. Glenn was certain. As far as college football went, Alabama might not be as good this year. Then again, they probably would be. They were due for an upset though.

Life ambled on, and by the time Thursday's shift arrived Joe was beginning to forget the tall man. He had other things to worry about. Joanne's carpal tunnel was acting up. Old Man Moore had abandoned his signal for number one and gone back to flipping his invisible birdy. If the suits up front didn't sell something, the plant might have a shutdown in September. It had happened before.

Joe almost had another week in the books by Friday, and after dinner breaks he made his rounds and gave out paychecks. It was the job Joe enjoyed most. Not only were the paychecks pleasant- although expected- news, he got a chance to chit-chat with each of his employees. He did care about each of them, almost as if they were his children.

Luther, with his bald head covered by a ball cap that had nothing on its front – the man who could make a three tone sound of train whistle-, always told him what he planned to do first with the money. T.J., a tiny man with a tiny voice and enormous black beard (most people thought he colored it with store-bought dye), usually thanked him and acknowledged "Well, it is that time of week". At least he smiled. The young guys folded the checks and stuffed them into pockets and sometimes mumbled, "Thanks".

When only one check remained, Joe walked to his car, sat inside, and studied the deductions and the result before placing it in his glove box. Then, he leaned back and wondered what he and Michelle might have done on the weekend if she was still around. That's what he was doing when Al pecked on his window.

"Al!" Joe said, surprised. He climbed out of the vehicle.

"How's it going, Joe?"

"Fine. Fine, Al. I, well, you know after the other night –"

"Thought you were imagining me or something?"

"Yes. That's right. I did. I get so tired on midnights."

"Well, T.G.I.F.," Al said. "But, after all, isn't every day the Lord's Day."

They laughed and then Joe said, "You're out early again. Not as early as last time, but early."

"Couldn't sleep. I don't sleep. I have plenty of my own work to do." He turned and sat on the edge of Joe's old, silver Caprice and folded his arms as he leaned back. "So, give it any more thought?"

"What's that?" Joe asked.

"Oh, don't tell me you've forgotten already. Vandy. The championship."

"That's funny. I did think about that. Funny stuff."

"Oh, Joe. It's not funny. It's reality."

Joe looked squarely into Al's face and found not one hint of humor.

"Joe," Al continued, "you, I, we can make this happen. I know you want it."

"It's been a long week, Al. You're going to have to be a little more to the point. I'm not with you."

"Joe, you give me what I want. I give you the chance of a lifetime. The chance to do what you've always dreamed of doing. The chance to give your team a championship to boot."

Joe's pulse began to race. What was this man saying? He thought he knew, but the proposition was almost unbelievable. He pinched his leg and tried to breathe. It certainly seemed as though he was awake, but he was beginning to wonder.

"What's my end of the deal?"

"I think we both know," Al said, laughing and rising to his full height from the edge of the car. "It's not as sinister as it sounds. You always wanted to play football. Didn't you."

In fact, Joe did. He played in high school. Well, that was being kind, because he didn't get to play much. At 5'10" tall and 160 pounds at the time, pretty slow, and not very strong, he usually watched from the sidelines as Doug Brown carried the ball. It wasn't much better for defense either. He was behind Terry Smith at free safety. He tried to kick but didn't have the leg strength. He *had* always wanted to play football.

"Your back's not what it used to be either, is it."

How could Al have known that? His back had never felt right after he strained it moving a mold one evening. It hurt when he awoke and every time he worked in the yard.

"I couldn't play now even if I wanted to," Joe said.

"Oh yes, yes you could. And you could awaken feeling like you did when you were eighteen. Remember that? You could be young again, and so strong this time."

"Al, no man can give me back what time has taken away."

"Go home at quitting time," Al said. He turned as if to walk away. "I'll be by to see you. I think I know where you live. We'll discuss it then."

Joe thought about what he usually did on Friday mornings. He always went to the bank and made a deposit with the teller Mary. Then, he often went to Hardee's and had a biscuit and gravy and talked with some of the men sitting around drinking coffee and solving the world's problems. How did Al know where he lived?

"Don't go to the bank," Al said. "Go straight home. It could change your life."

Al began to walk away and looking over his shoulder gave Joe a wink and a smile. Joe turned his head back to the plant and when he turned back to cast his gaze over the parking lot once more, Al was nowhere in sight. Joe jogged in the direction Al had walked, and then, even though it was slow and more painful than when he used to run a little, he hurried across the lot. Al was nowhere to be found.

Back inside the plant the presses chugged, molding plastic, making parts, and creating new things seemingly from nothing. Glenn buzzed by on a tow motor to fill the last of the hoppers one more time. Joe moved out of the way, dazed, and staggered into the supervisor's office where he shut the door behind him. He sat in a rolling chair and leaned back thinking about Al. Was he being asked to give up his soul? What could it mean? And even though he had done nothing wrong, Joe felt a pang of guilt.

After the last of the employees packed up and left and Joe had finally managed to square away the week's work, he ambled to the parking lot. He started the car and sat inside for a bit letting the air conditioner begin to work. Looking to the glove box, he considered the check inside and then thought about going to Hardee's. What could it hurt? He could always deposit the check on Monday. He was tired. Maybe he needed to rest, because his encounter with Al had to be some kind of crazy dream, a trick his mind was playing. When he thought back on it later, he realized he never even remembered driving home, but he made it and stumbled inside and into his recliner. He had begun to doze when he heard the sound.

Al had cleared his throat.

Chapter 3

"I hope you don't mind. I showed myself in."

"No, no, I guess not," Joe said, disoriented. He sat up on the couch, looking up at the tall man standing in front of him. He was dressed the same as he was when Joe first met him. His tan face made him look like a game show host.

"Let's get down to the nitty gritty. Shall we?" Al walked to the nearby dining area, grabbed a chair, and sat it in front of Joe before moving the table somewhat. He produced a sheet of paper. "You sign right here," he said pointing to the bottom line on the paper as Joe tried to rub his eyes free of the short sleep, "and you become the greatest college football player to ever play the game."

"I'm not even in school much less on the team. Practice starts Monday."

"Oh, Joe," Al said smiling. "You don't give me nearly enough credit."

"They might know me."

"You're already enrolled in classes. Made great grades and the ACT was a breeze. Twelve hours is plenty for a freshman. You went to school at McMinn, but you didn't even play. You'll walk on. Your uncle paid for school."

Joe's head was spinning. Was this a dream? It had to be.

"It's been so long," Joe said. He craned his neck to see the paper, but Al moved it out of the way. "I won't remember the moves. I don't know if I could play."

"Joe, the way you'll play will be by instinct. It will come so naturally you won't believe it. You can do it all. Don't you feel it? You feel like an All-American already, don't you."

In fact, Joe did feel it already. Something was happening. He shook his head and tried to think. What about work? What about his current life? Now the change was noticeable, as if his skin grew tight. The ringing in his ears, brought on either by age or the constant roar of the presses in the plant, began to disappear, replaced by an eerie silence. He heard the movement of cloth on cloth as he repositioned his legs. Even his right ear that had been fading for the last decade detected Al's lips sliding over teeth as he smiled.

"The house is paid for," Al said. He was so convincing? It all fell into place so easily. "Why would you worry about this life? Your new one awaits. Go look in the mirror. Go on."

Joe rose and walked to the guest bathroom, flicked on the light, and realized at once the face in the mirror was unrecognizable. He had a full head of Leonardo DiCaprio hair only more blonde, curly and thick. His cheek bones sat high, his face taut and perfectly sallow, while one side of his full lips curled in a distinctive and not altogether unattractive quirk, the only distinguishing Cain-like mark on his otherwise perfect appearance. His neck muscles fell onto thick, high shoulder muscles. How could this be?

"Al, how can this be?" Joe said walking back to the living room. Al leaned back, his arms crossed across his chest.

"You ask too many questions. Look, your bag is packed and ready."

A suitcase on rollers with a pull handle sat beside the door.

"I can't give my life away, just like this. It's all too sudden."

Al breathed deeply and stood again as Joe sat on the edge of the couch, placing his hands on his knees and then rubbing them up his muscular legs.

"My God, you drive a hard bargain," Al said. "Can I say that, Joe?" Al laughed before continuing. "One hundred days. We'll try it for one hundred days. At that point, you'll make the deal: go back to work like it never happened or continue on with your amazing season. You know I can do it. I think my work thus far proves that."

One hundred days. He could live the life he had always dreamed of and Vandy could at least have him for that long. He could try this thing out for one hundred days. What could it hurt?

"One hundred days." Joe looked to the bag and back to Al. "What is my end of the deal, exactly?"

"It doesn't really matter does it? You're under no obligation to do anything in return unless you accept in one hundred days."

For the first time in so many years, Joe felt it: the unmistakable pull of an invisible longing, the rending of what seemed right with what seemed wrong, and the inevitable decision to experiment and stick in a toe to test the waters. But there was a division. Oh yes, there was something about this that was so very wrong, and the voice in Joe's head screamed for him to snap out of this impossible dream, this ridiculous musing that had been held at bay for so, so many years. What was his crime though? What was it really? Who was holding him responsible for this decision and who had been that authority in charge when Michelle was in peril?

"A limo awaits. I think freshmen are moving into the dorms. You need to introduce yourself to Coach Michaels tomorrow. You have a big day ahead."

Joe couldn't move. He wanted to go and he wanted to stay at the same time.

"Go ahead. Enjoy."

Joe walked across the room, grabbed the handle of the bag, and opened the door. Sure enough, a black limo with tinted windows sat in front of the house. He didn't even bother to lock the door as he left the house.

Chapter 4

The back door opened slowly on its own, and Joe peered inside letting his eyes adjust. He lowered the handle on the suitcase and tossed the bag into the floor before climbing inside and sliding across the curving black, plush and rounded seat that spanned several feet. The door shut behind him. When he felt the limo begin to move he thought for a moment there might not even be anyone driving, which wouldn't have been surprising after all that had happened so far. But a closer look revealed the outline of a driver's head in the front. Soft music surrounded him.

Joe opened the door of a small refrigerator and found it stocked with all sorts of beverages.

"Take whatever you wish," a voice from a speaker inside the limo said. Joe selected a bottle of water.

What would they think at the plant when he didn't show up for work on Sunday? Who would start the presses? Joe tried to get comfortable inside the womb of the limo, but his sense of responsibility became a nagging buzz that wouldn't stop. He hadn't signed anything yet. He could go back, right now, and things would be as they were. He could still do it. Yet, it was only Friday. Maybe he would see how things progressed over the weekend.

Joe decided to have a look inside his bag. He leaned over and unzipped the side pocket where he found a billfold first. Taking it out and opening it, he found several one-hundred dollar bills inside. Now that was a booster. An image from the driver's license inside a clear plastic covering caught his eye. It was the face he had seen in the mirror. It was him.

Joey Goodman. That was his name. He needed to remember it. 5'11". 185 pounds. Blonde hair, blue eyes. He was 18 years old and would be 19 in late August. Kindergarten redshirt? He guessed so.

Inside the front pocket Joey found his housing information and Monday's freshman orientation schedule. Suite 213. Fitting.

The limo stopped and this time the driver, a hunching man with a black hat pulled over the top of his face, came around and opened the door.

"If you need Mr. Appel, you need only look," he said and then moved at once back to the front, climbed inside, and drove away leaving Joey standing on the curb in front of the Leamon Dorm. He took a deep breath and walked to the entrance.

Students bustled by in the sparse lobby, and Joey stood there not knowing quite what to do. He had a bag and nothing else, but all around him other students were carrying refrigerators, microwaves, and an odd assortment of all the things needed to make a home. His head spun.

"Can I help you?" a girl behind a table on the far side of the room asked.

"I'm in 213. Joey Goodman. Who do I need to see?"

The girl dug around in a box labeled with names sorted in alphabetical order. After she found his packet, she produced a key and explained how to get inside the dorm (until he could get an ID made, then he had to slide the card) and where everything was located. Clearly she had recited her script many times before.

"Take the elevator. Second floor, then go right. They're labeled. Welcome to Vanderbilt." The girl grinned so big that had she been a cartoon a twinkling spot of starlight would have sparkled on her teeth.

The elevator smelled of sweat and cologne, and as the door opened on the second floor he heard yells and laughter from down the hall. It looked as though his room was near the end.

Joe expected to see a barren room, or boxes and chaos in the midst of moving when he entered, but instead he found subdued light and a student reading at a table with a small light. The young man looked up from his book, his hair standing up on end from the back of his head like an antennae as if he might have been lying in bed in the recent past. He pushed a pair of black glasses up from the end of his nose.

"Hey," he said. "You must be Joey."

"Yeah, Joey Goodman. You must be my roommate?"

"Right." He waved somewhat and then sat there, not resuming his reading but looking at Joey. "My stuff's here. Been here all summer. I had to get an early start. My dad made me."

"That's good. Good," Joey said surveying his new home.

"Name's Tyler. Tyler Cobb. Your people came by and brought your stuff," Tyler said. "It's all in place. Nice TV by the way."

"Yeah," Joey said. He had no idea how to answer. He had never seen the television.

"Your room," Tyler said pointing. He didn't say anything else, but he didn't turn around to read again. Tyler might have wanted to say more but didn't know how, lost somewhere between books and learning and the real world.

"Right. Okay then. I'll, uh, drop this bag," Joey said. He left Tyler and walked into the room. The bed was made. Dark sheets and pillow cases. A lamp. A computer. A clock set to the correct time. Books, including a thesaurus, dictionary, handbook of allusions, *Harbrace Handbook*, and some reference volumes Joey wasn't familiar with. He sat on the bed. Somewhere down the hall he could hear muted voices. What in the world was he doing? How could this be happening?

Joey fell back on the bed and looked to the ceiling in the dim light. He closed his eyes and thought of Michelle. The sounds faded and he slept.

Since there were no windows in Joey's room, he didn't have any way to know how late it was until he glanced at the clock and discovered it was past five. He was fiercely hungry though. Tyler wasn't in the common area of the suite, so Joey went alone in search of food, preferably pizza from Joe Daily's favorite joint on the other side of the campus. He had become Joey so recently he almost didn't notice when two co-eds walking in the opposite direction smiled. One of them twirled a long lock of dishwater blonde hair as she did so. They were young enough to be his daughters, but here he was in a young, strong body. In his own opinion Al had made him considerably more attractive as well.

It had been years since he could eat the way he did at the pizzeria. He devoured an entire small pizza and still felt as if he could eat more. But as he thought about his first day of school on Monday and maybe his only shot at making an impression with the coach, he decided he had eaten enough. The thought of his situation made his appetite vanish anyway.

The evening was already cooling somewhat and his stroll back in the direction of the dorm was pleasant. Students sat in the shade talking. Some passed Frisbees. A football game had begun at Marler Field, and Joey decided to stop and watch. He didn't watch long until he was invited to play. *Okay, Al, let's see what this body is all about.*

Joey's team didn't seem nearly as talented as the opposition, if looking at the players was any indication. Most of the guys knew each other though, so maybe they had been divided equally. His team got the ball first. Two hands below the waist. Some things never changed.

After one of his chubby, slow teammates was tagged on the return, Joey split out wide. It was time to see what kind of speed he had. He ran a fly on the first play, and his man fell behind at once, but the quarterback threw an incomplete pass into the flat. Obviously Joey was too far away and too deep for any pass attempt. He did have speed, spectacular speed in fact, but after he was ignored on two more plays, the ball got punted out of bounds.

Pairing off to cover different men, the defensive series went much like offense had. Passes went in different directions and ball carriers were tagged near the line. The game so far was boring by anyone's standards. Then things took an interesting turn.

"Mikey, you can't even throw the ball," the captain said.

"The rush is so fast no one's open," Mikey argued. "None of you block."

"Who can quarterback? You ever quarterback?" captain asked Joey.

"I can give it a whirl," Joey said.

Routes were designed and players flanked out wide and close. Joey's first actual play had arrived.

The snap came back to him in the shotgun and two defenders rushed and were on him in an instant. Joey turned and dodged then sprinted away easily as he looked downfield for an open man. Players streaked right and left. One man ran a post, angling far across the field to the left as Joey moved right. He planted, reached back, and as if by instinct fired his pass. The ball was a rocket, whizzing with an audible buzz, and hit the receiver literally in the middle of the chest. He dropped it then rubbed where the ball had struck him.

"Catch the ball!" captain screamed. "What a pass."

In the huddle players struggled to catch their breath, sweat pouring in the warm evening. Joey seemed to have little or no ill effects from the weather or the exertion.

"Do it again," Joey said. "Same patterns."

Instead of looking downfield so much, Joey had an idea. *Greatest player ever, huh?* He would see for himself.

Joey took the snap, and this time evaded easily to the left. He pumped a pass to a receiver, feigned looking downfield, and began to sprint. The players close to him fell behind at once. Defenders left the receivers and pursued. He juked and another player fell to his side. Another move and two remained between him and the open field and end zone. Instead of making another move, he planted and sprinted in the opposite direction. Five yards and then ten. No one was even close. He raced to the end zone. His team was in the lead.

"Great run!" captain screamed. "No extra points. You scored. You kick off."

As it has been done for years in the sandlot, the kick off was actually a punt. Joey held the ball, surveyed his defenders, and punted with all his might. The ball arced high in the air in a perfect spiral, far over everyone's head and through the end zone.

"Do you play for the team?" someone said.

Joey shook his head. He might not now but it sure looked like he would be in the near future.

Joey made two "tackles" on the next defensive set, and then the other team's best player caught a pass far away on the other side of the field. Joey tracked him down and caught him around what would have been the ten yard line. Two hands below the waist.

"I scored. You didn't get me," the player said. "The tag was high."

"Not even close!" captain said. "He got you."

"Now, you're going to cheat," the player said.

The score was tied. Joey said nothing, but retreated and waited on the kickoff, which Joey took on the fly. He weaved in and out of the defense and went into the end zone again untouched. On the ensuing kickoff, Joey kicked the ball through the end zone as he had before.

In almost the exact same situation as the time before, the other team's scoring player caught a pass once more, this time not quite so far away but behind the defense nonetheless. Joey unleashed his speed, but deciding on a different tactic ran ahead at a slightly different angle. He wouldn't come in from behind this time. He circled in front. And instead of tagging below the waist, Joey broke down and scooped the player into the air and set him down softly on his back. Then he tagged him, two hands, one on each leg.

"This isn't tackle," the player screamed, scrambling to his feet. He came nose to nose with Joey who held his ground. As if he sensed Joey wouldn't back down and clearly outmuscled, he froze. "I'm through, man." He began walking away.

"You baby!" the captain of Joey's team screamed.

But the game was over.

"Where did you learn to play?"

"It's kind of a gift," Joey said. No truer words had ever been spoken. It wasn't a gift however. This talent came at a price.

"You should try out for the team."

"You think so?" Joey asked. "Maybe I will."

His first foray into college competition had been on a small scale, but it proved much to Joey. He *did* have skills. Major skills. If he decided to go through with this, things were going to get very interesting.

Chapter 5

The pool table in the commons room of the dorm was a hot attraction. Most of the guys staying in the dorm and not holding a cue stick were either sitting in chairs watching the action or standing around cheering. Joey tried to learn everyone's name but mostly sat out of the way trying to be inconspicuous. Kevin must have been a hot name a few years ago, because the dorm had three of them and each loved playing pool but weren't very good. The conversation was so lively, getting lost in the flow to become one of the guys proved to be easy. Joey's mind kept wandering to a meeting with Coach Michaels. How was he going to pull this off even with Al's help?

"You new?"

Joey looked up to see a tall African-American man, muscular, in a tank top and shorts. He looked as though he would be outstanding at anything involving athletics. Even the way he stood, with an ethereal tilt of the hip, screamed athlete.

"Yeah. Name's Joey." He offered his hand and the other student shook it.

"My first year here too. I'm Willy."

Joey looked back to the game of pool and felt completely out of his element. The young man stood there beside him, watching the games himself, but altogether more confident and put together than Joey.

"You look like you could play football," Joey said.

"Yeah, that's the plan. I hope so. I'm going over later today to meet Michaels. He doesn't know I'm here."

"Really?"

"Yeah, I thought maybe I could walk on. I keep getting the run around when I call, so I'm going to go over and introduce myself. I don't know any other way."

"So you play? Or you played?"

"Man, it's a long story. I played for Memphis three years ago. I got this." Willy raised his shirt and in the middle of a serious six-pack that would have been the envy of any bodybuilder sat a scar about six inches long, discolored, and still nasty looking even though it was healed.

"Playing?"

"Man, I told you it was a long story. I wasn't playing. I was, I was taking up for a girl. It wasn't my fault, but I still got it following me around."

"Well, I hope you make the team, Willy," Joe said.

"These chumps can't play pool," he said.

Joey realized what Willy had said, not referring to pool but that he was going over to the field later to see Michaels. The team was already practicing and had been for a while. It didn't even seem likely that walk-ons would be permitted at this late date. What didn't seem likely, though, was that Joey could look into the mirror and not see Joe.

"Hey, can I walk over with you?" Joey asked.

Willy agreed and said he'd meet Joey in an hour, and when the hour passed and Willy still hadn't shown he was almost ready to go back up to his room, even though the prospect of watching part of a practice was alluring. But finally, Willy did show. He carried cleats and a bag.

"You got cleats too?" Willy asked, noticing that Joey was also carrying some things. "You gonna try out?"

"I dunno. Maybe. We might pass a ball around or something, you know. You might need for me to help."

"That's fine. Chill. It's all good," Willy said.

They walked toward the practice field, near Marler where Joey had put on the football exhibition, and more than once Willy breathed deep and exhaled audibly. Joey finally had enough and had to ask what he was doing.

"What?"

"I mean the deep breathing. What is it?" Joey asked.

"Man, I'm so nervous. I've never been this nervous."

"Why are you nervous? You've played college football. It's not like you don't know what to expect."

They crossed a road and turned left and could see the field in the distance.

"My Gra-ma wanted me to come here. I want to be a lawyer, and I can do the work. It's a hard school. It's great preparation. I've always wanted to play football though. Man, if I don't get a chance, I'll never live with myself."

"Then do your best. Michaels will certainly let you play if you're good enough. He's a good man, I mean from all I can tell."

Willy nodded and continued walking, looking straight ahead, lips pursed. It seemed there was more to this than Joey knew. He wasn't about to press the matter right now though.

"So they let people watch practice? I've never tried to come over and watch. I thought it was probably closed."

"They let anyone watch, at least until the season starts. There aren't too many people there. Some girlfriends and some other girls. Some guys that think they can play college football. I think there are usually some reporters standing around that cover the team."

Sure enough, when they got near the practice field, there were very few people watching. The small stands were virtually empty and anyone could walk up to the edge of the practice field and stand if they had a notion to do so. The only thing keeping spectators away from the field was an invisible boundary of respect.

They sat on the first row of the small, aluminum stands and watched drills. Willy had spotted Michaels with the linemen, and he didn't take his eyes off the man. Willy's intensity was almost unnerving. He must have been something before the stabbing.

Whistles blew and players moved. A large digital clock with red numerals ticked on the far side of the field. And before Joey realized practice had even concluded Willy was on his feet moving fast.

"Wish me luck," he yelled over his shoulder.

Willy spoke to a pair of players as he trotted across the field, and when he got to the far side he stood behind two coaches who had begun talking to Michaels. The head coach was a big man, easily as tall as Willy and twice as big around. He had been a lineman in college. The coach was smart too. Whether he was smart enough to eventually raise the Commodores to competitive status was yet to be decided.

"Walk over there," someone behind Joey said.

Joey turned around and saw Al leaning back, relaxed with his arms crossed on his chest.

"I didn't know you were there."

"I am. Go over there. Tell him you want to help the team."

"Really?"

"Go," Al said, flicking his wrist as if shooing Joey in that direction.

Joey made it to Willy when the coach finally broke free.

"Willy?"

"Hi coach. I'm Willy-"

"I know who you are. How ya' doing?" Michaels asked.

"I'm good. I'm healed."

"Good. Good for you. What brings you to practice?"

"I'm in school. I mean, here. I'm in school here at Vandy. I want to play football."

The comment stopped Michaels' banter. Suddenly serious, he surveyed Willy and then looked away. Joey, who had walked up behind the pair, thought that couldn't be a good sign.

"Willy, we've already started practice. I've got my walk-ons."

"I just want a chance," Willy said.

Michaels said nothing, searching as if he didn't know how to reply. Then he looked around at Joey.

"Who's this? You want to try out too?"

"I think I could maybe help the team," Joey said. Isn't that what Al said to say?

"You look like a kicker. You kick?"

"Sure. I can do anything."

"You can?"

The coach looked around and spotted a rack of footballs the managers hadn't corralled yet and walked over picking up one in his big paw.

"Here. Kick this ball to Willy. Run down to the other end, Willy."

Willy ran about forty yards down the field and turned around. Joey remembered the previous evening and motioned for Willy to back up, and when he backed up ten more yards he motioned again. Joey took one step and punted. The ball arced high in a spiral, over Willy's head, sending him back at a full sprint, more than twenty more yards. Willy did manage to catch it over his shoulder gracefully.

"You a soccer player?"

"No sir. I used to play a little football in the backyard."

"Again." He tossed Joey another football. Joey repeated his kick even deeper. "I don't think I've seen anyone punt a ball that deep. Ever. You must've had a big back yard."

Michaels was smiling.

"This must be my lucky day, if you can do that under pressure."

"I think I can play anywhere," Joey said.

The coach motioned for Willy to come back, and when he did it seemed the coach had come to a solution.

"Willy, you come by my office tomorrow afternoon at two. You," he said pointing to Joey, "come by practice Monday. Be at the field house at three."

And with that he walked away, a rotund wobbling stroll into the evening toward the field house.

Joey and Willy stood there for a moment and then finally walked back to get their things out of the stands.

"I think we're in," Joey said.

Willy was not so optimistic.

"Not good," Willy said. "I get this feeling."

"Man, going back for the ball, I've seen grace before and you have it. I want to see you playing for Vandy. You can play."

"Where'd you learn to punt like that? You didn't tell me you were a kicker."

"It's a gift. I can play. We can play. He'll take you; I know it."

"We'll see," Willy said. "We'll see."

Al was nowhere in sight when they got their bags, which was just as well. He was beginning to give Joey the creeps. He didn't want to be thinking about Al, because today was cause for celebration. Joey broke one of Al's hundreds and they had pizza, comfort food that no amount of worry could withstand.

Chapter 6

Joey could hear Tyler pecking on a keyboard inside his bedroom throughout the day, and once as he lay in bed reading he heard the commode flush. Joey didn't visibly see his roommate all day though. After contemplating asking Tyler if he wanted to go out for dinner, he abandoned the idea and roamed around the hall and into what he was now calling the pool room. It was vacant as well. Even Willy never answered repeated knocks on his door.

Late in the afternoon Joey decided it was time to phone in sick. He hadn't found a phone in his bag – which was surprising all things considered – so he went downstairs to use the phone in the lobby to call the plant.

When he began entering digits a hand reached around, seized the phone, and put it back into its cradle. Al stood behind him.

"You can't call," Al said before stepping back and then sitting reluctantly on the edge of a dirty, brown chair.

"I have to tell them I won't be there," Joey said. His fear and doubt, that little nagging voice in his mind that told him this was not right and not good, was screaming again. The voice said it still wasn't too late.

"Joey, you're in now. Let's play this thing for all it's worth. One hundred days."

Joey looked around the deserted lobby and down to the floor before mustering the courage to face Al once more. He wasn't sure if he was scared or doubtful. Things were happening so fast.

"I don't think I can do this," he said finally.

"Let's walk. Come on." Al smiled, happy to be moving and out of the chair. Happy to be with Joey. Life was grand.

They left the lobby and began across the campus as night fell around them. Neither said anything for a bit, and when they came to a large cement median which was the base for a gazing statue of a well dressed man studying the expansive campus, they took a seat.

"You'll be fine," Al said.

Joey said nothing wondering how to make his argument. He had almost decided he didn't want it. It wasn't worth it. Then again, he didn't know for certain what his end of the deal was exactly. There was much that he could demand if this were indeed real. Why though? Why him?

"You know, Joey," Al began, "God could do this for everyone. Everyone could be young. You believe that, don't you?"

"I guess I do. Yeah, I believe it." After he said it, Joey realized that he did indeed believe it, and the thought made him angry. That old drive, the one he harbored when he had been a young man, surfaced once more, and all the years of work and pain and sorrow came to mind. God was omnipotent and could do anything, yet…

"Ever wonder why there's so much suffering in the world? Why does He let that happen?"

Joey remained silent. He didn't have an answer. Al continued.

"You know what's worse? He can conquer death. He can. No one has to die."

The comment struck home, and Joey thought of Michelle as he looked directly in Al's face. No one had to die. Not Michelle. Not anyone. Now he was no longer angry, but infuriated beyond measure. He could do this, and what's more he would do this. What did he have to lose? Many times it seemed as though he had already lost everything.

"I made you young," Al said. "You think I can conquer death?"

The point had been made. Was there more that could be done? There were further possibilities, or at least it seemed that way for Joey. The question was could he save Michelle?

"One hundred days. To decide. One hundred days?" Al looked to the heavens before continuing. "That was the deal, Joey. No one can know though. Do you understand? No one. My end of the deal is off if anyone finds out."

Joey felt the chill of the threat as it coursed through his veins. He didn't even dare to contemplate what might happen if someone did find out. And, he felt a bit of shame, for backing out on his friend Al and yet paradoxically for even going through with Al's plan. What crime had he committed though? What was wrong with pursuing a course of action that would make him happy? What was so wrong with being given contentment?

"Now," Al said, "let's head back and get ready to live. Really live. Enjoy this thing. It's going to be amazing; it really is."

Al went his way when they neared the dorm, and Joey retreated inside. In the morning he attended the first class of the orientation, wondering all the while how to escape back to his room. Even though he watched for Willy, he never spotted him all day. That afternoon, he ventured to the field house, and found he was the only player there at three.

Joey pecked on Coach Michael's closed door, and after hearing a muffled answer opened it slowly to peer inside.

"Joey!" Michaels said with genuine enthusiasm. "Have a seat."

The coach took a folder from his desk and sat precariously on the wooden top as he opened it.

"We got your file. You're all set. I thought we'd have to go clearinghouse then get a physical, but you're all set. You have one heck of a guidance counselor."

"I do at that," Joey said. He thought of Al.

"Never played in high school? Why not?"

"I, uh, I worked."

"Says your father is self-employed."

"Yes sir, he was. I worked for my father." Joey wasn't certain it was the first lie he had told since all this started, but he was fairly certain it wouldn't be the last.

"McMinn doesn't know what it was missing," Michaels said. He studied Joey for a moment. "Okay, guys will start getting here and getting taped up any time now. Go to the trainer. Get pads. Meet on the field at four for stretching. Sound good?"

"I guess so."

"Okay then. Now, this is sort of a tryout, I guess you could call it. Let's see how it goes."

Easy as that, Joey began his career at Vandy. The trainers and the managers fixed him up with pads, a number 99 jersey along with football pants, and then fitted him with a helmet complete with the mask he requested. For a super fan like Joey, who used to be Joe, the entire treatment was like fantasy camp.

An NCAA head coach is more like the CEO of a corporation, and planning has to be meticulous in order to cover everything a team needs to cover in only twenty hours per week of practice. Michaels was no different. Joey was amazed at the preparation and the team's workload, but his own practices all through the week consisted of punting and working on kicking drills. Most of the assistants' time was being spent on proven commodities though, and through Thursday he had only kicked a few times, all beautiful, long kicks but yet unnoticed.

Practices were crisp with final run-throughs on offense and defense, and with only one week remaining the team had already begun preparation for their opener with Western Kentucky, a non-conference game against a team they were expected to handle easily. Joey watched and learned.

Classes began on Friday, and his friend Willy who had opened the door to being on the team was nowhere to be found. He never answered knocks on the door of his dorm room, and he never ventured out to the doughnut shop or anywhere the guys went in the evening. Joey had three classes on Monday, Wednesday, and Friday, and while he walked to each class he searched faces. It seemed as though Willy had vanished.

But at practice on Saturday, the day that Joey would finally get a break on the team, he spotted Willy who gave a half-hearted wave from the stands. There had to be some way he could repay his friend. It was obvious the wide receivers were nowhere close to being as talented.

During live punting action, Vandy's number one punter came up lame. When coaches looked for the number two punter and couldn't locate him quickly, Joey ran onto the field, helmet strapped and ready.

"I'll do it, coach," Joey said.

"Okay, full speed. Here we go."

Joey took the snap and boomed a high, spiraling punt all the way to the other ten where the team's fastest player took the ball in an ill-advised catch over his shoulder. He quickly remedied that mistake though when he circled back left and began accelerating away from the defenders. Soon, Joey was the only one standing in the way of a score. As the player juked, Joey exploded into his legs and upended him in a violent collision.

Running the punt play again, Joey tracked the ball carrier once more and ran him down from the side, tackling him with ease. Michaels blew his whistle.

"You have no problem tackling an All-SEC returner," the coach said. "Stick around after practice. I want to time you."

And that was how Joey began his odyssey of playing time.

"Forty yards," Michaels said.

As all the other players made their way to the locker room, Michaels sent a coach downfield with his stopwatch. The lights from the field shone like a harsh interrogation as darkness began settling over Nashville.

"He'll go on your first movement," Michaels said. "Run through him. Don't slow down."

Joey noticed Willy still sitting in the stands.

"I need someone to run with me," Joey said. "How 'bout Willy over there."

Michaels looked to the stands then back to Joey, seemingly turning the idea over in his mind. He motioned for Willy.

"I'll time you. Anthony will get Willy. First movement and you both go." Willy arrived. "Can you run a couple of these with Joey?"

"Sure," Willy said, already changing into his cleats and stretching. He hopped up and down a few times as Michaels went to the other end. "Thanks man."

"No problem. I wouldn't be out here if it wasn't for you."

"I'm sorry I've been ignoring you," Willy said.

"Run fast."

When Joey and Willy were ready, they each eased down into a three-point stance. Willy dug one foot into the turf.

"On three we go. You ready?"

"Let's do this," Willy whispered.

"One… two… three!"

Joey knew what he had on his side, but he never expected the type of explosion out of his stance that Willy demonstrated. In only two steps, Joey was behind. There would be no need to hold back. Joey accelerated and caught Willy near the thirty yard line and then with a bit more effort pulled away, finishing a full two steps in front.

"I don't think we got it," Michaels said. "Let's go again."

Joey and Willy trotted back to their spots trying to catch their breath.

"I think he did get it," Joey said under his breath and looking away. "That was fast."

"Man, I have to do this."

"You will. You count this time."

When they screamed out of their stances this time, Joey did not hold back. He saw Willy just behind him, a long, hulking figure, pulling with all his might. The coaches were a blur as the pair of wood-be players raced by. When they walked back, both of the coaches were smiling. Michaels held his watch as if he was afraid the time might fall away and be lost forever.

"I've never seen a time like that. Willy was at 4.28. You're the fastest player I've ever seen, Joey."

"Thanks coach," Joey said. He had already caught his breath. "I told you, I want to help the team. I can play anywhere and everywhere. He can help us too."

They all three looked at Willy.

"You want us both? On Monday?" Joey asked.

"Come to my office. Tomorrow. Two. Both of you. We have some work to do."

That evening's pizza was on Willy. They had lots of learning to do in a short amount of time. It would take teamwork for them to pull this off.

Leaving the field, if they had looked to the far end zone, they would have noticed Al, standing like Bear Bryant leaning against the goal post. He wasn't smiling.

Chapter 7

The dorm had characters sprinkled throughout, and each of them had a story. There was Eddie Violet, the muscular boxer who oddly enough played trumpet in the band. His tall roommate, also in the band, was a tobacco farmer who had raised 4H chickens each year since he was eight. There was Kevin Miller, a blond guitar player from Indiana who never slept. Then there was Kevin Brown, who was already being called "Downtown Kevin Brown", weighing in at well over 300 pounds and standing 6'2". Downtown liked to knit, listen to '80s music, and he drove a white Chevy pickup truck that was smaller than he was and leaned to the left as he careened through the downtown area of Music City.

It was a safe bet none of them had a history like Willy's.

"So tell me the story," Joey said to Willy as they sat in the pizzeria watching Sports Center and eavesdropping on the locals.

"What story?"

"The long story. You said it was long story. You can tell me."

"I'd rather not. It's not good conversation," Willy said. He looked to the television screen.

Joey sat and waited. He didn't ask again, but he didn't say anything else either. Finally, Willy turned around and faced his friend.

"Please don't repeat it. I know anyone can find out. I mean, people might already know. I'm certain Vandy does already."

"I'm not going to say anything."

"Okay, the scar. When I was at Memphis, I used to go run around at night. I'm not much of a drinker. I never have. I don't care if people drink, really, but I do like to get out and go to clubs. Meet the ladies. That sort of thing.

"I'm out one night. On Beale Street. It's really late. Things are gettin' freaky. I'm gettin' tired. I decide to cut out. I go outside and I walk by this alley, and there's this guy. He's got this girl pushed up against a wall, and I can see it's not good, you know? He's got his forearm on her neck, and he's pointing his finger right in her face. I can't hear them, but I see her face. She's shrinking back from him. She's crying. Scared as hell. So I yell 'Hey, stop!', but he didn't even hear me. He's enraged.

"I go down the alley and yell again. I said 'Leave her alone'. I get right up on them before he looks at me. His eyes are crazy. He's crazy. I pushed him away, and before I know it he comes at me, grabs me, tries to hit me and I block a punch or two. I get his shirt and spin him down, away from me, on the ground. He comes right back up. I think I hit him once, but he kept coming." Willie paused, lost in thought as if he was reliving the moment. Then he continued. "He grabs me around the neck, kind of with his whole arm, and we're tangled up. I remember this 'click' sound, and then it was like fire, right in the middle of my stomach.

"I doubled over and they were gone. My hand is full of blood. There's people coming into the alley, people screaming. God, I was bleeding so bad. Then, there's an ambulance. I wake up in the hospital. They said I was going to live, but, you know, everybody's acting so weird."

"So you tried to help and the guy cut you? Why is that bad?"

"I'm not finished. So, the second or third day, this detective comes in and wants to ask me questions. I figured they're going to try to catch this guy who cut me, who beat up this girl. He wants to know what happened, and I told him. Then he says the girl told him I was raping her. Her 'boyfriend' had stepped in to stop me. That's what she's saying. When I finally got out of the hospital, they arrest me, book me, take me to jail.

"By the time I get things cleared up, in court, I've lost my scholarship, a half year of school, and I'm out of there. I was innocent. The charges were dropped. There wasn't even a trial. The guy goes free, Joey. He never does a day. I have my life ruined. All because I tried to help. I didn't try to rape anyone, Joey."

"Willy, I believe you."

"Joey, you don't know me. I appreciate it. But, you know, I just don't talk about it anymore. I know that's why Michaels was hesitant. I know tomorrow, he's going to give me an ultimatum, and I'm fine with that. I didn't do anything. I've never been in any trouble."

"Then let's move on. Fresh start. It's over."

"It'll never really be over. Joey, I could've already been on there." He motioned to the sports program.

Willy eased his chair back and looked at the TV screen and watched Sports Center, maybe imagining they were talking about him. A cloud had descended over him.

"I got recruited by everybody. Notre Dame, USC – out west not South Carolina, LSU, Alabama. Everybody. Grandma wanted me close to home. I went to Memphis. It's the biggest signing day, ever. Five star goes to Memphis. I can play close to home and make it. I know I can. Then the night. I should never have gone out that night."

They walked back to the dorm and went inside and up to Willy's room. No one was there, and they plopped down on the sofa and turned ESPN on again. Neither said much and finally Joey went back to his room to rest for tomorrow. It seemed as though the day would be big. They had much work to do.

When Joey and Willy got to Michaels' office, the team's quarterback, a redshirt sophomore named Ronnie Couch who had played in ten games last year and was more of a runner than a passer, and the team's All-SEC safety and return guy Mark Dennison , a senior from Gadsden, Alabama who was a pre-med major, sat waiting and watching film of Western Kentucky.

"Hey guys. We're going to spend some time with you two today," Couch said, locating a remote control and flipping off the tape.

"Joey, I guess they saw you pop me the other day," Dennison said. "I know I felt it. They're going to see if you can play. Even if you do really well this week you might not get much playing time unless we can get ahead, but they're going to look. Guys with your speed don't come along very often. You need to know at least a little bit about what to do on defense."

Dennison began at once explaining the basics of the Cover-2 defense, while Couch explained some basic plays for Willy, who would have a much easier time grasping enough to get playing time. The game was easier for wide receivers and Willy had played in college before. Then, the group began to run some plays, Joey covering Willy. While Joey struggled each time to be in position, he made up for many of his deficiencies with pure, raw athletic ability. Even when Willy used his long frame to go up for a high pass, Joey managed to get up in the air and disrupt almost every one.

After almost two hours on the field, Michaels and another coach walked out and led the group back inside. The coaches kept Joey and Willy and sent the other players on their way.

"You'll each get some reps this week. I doubt you'll get into the game. But I'm going to go ahead and send a playbook with you. I know classes start this week, but your load is just going to be heavier. You need to know this."

The coach dropped a blue three-ring binder containing the offensive set-up in front of Willy and the defensive white one in front of Joey. Then, Michaels handed them a plastic container filled with DVD's.

"Guard these. They don't get out of your sight. Understand?"

Both players nodded.

"See you at morning workout, and then at practice. Study. The DVD's give you a chance to watch almost any play and watch it run correctly. Joey, there are some coverage packages and technique sections you need to pay close attention to."

The Western Kentucky game was less than seven days away.

Chapter 8

Joey and Willy got a big send off Friday afternoon before they departed for the Hilton Garden Inn to spend the night with the team. They were the only two players who were not staying in the dorms allotted for official players, and their friends wanted to celebrate and wish them luck. Kevin Miller appeared first, carrying a lopsided cake smeared with white icing that was thin enough in places to see the cake beneath. Someone had written "Good Luck" in black and gold around one candle that burned on its top. A member of the guilty party knew a girl in a separate apartment that had a stove, and voila, a cake. Eight other guys followed behind Miller, most of them snickering, some of them discussing whether or not they should sing something.

Not only had classes started, Willy and Joey's football education had begun. Throughout the week, they had watched each of the sections of the video, memorizing plays and coverages. Then, late in the evening after each practice this week, they went outside and practiced moves and things they had learned. Often, their friends would come outside and toss a pass or help out. It was a team project, and by the end of the week the two players had begun to grasp many of the concepts. Joey had moved to number two on several of the defensive packages. If the coaches could have evaluated players on work from this week only, Willy would have been starting. For that matter, if they had known more about Joey, he would have been playing as well.

After a team meeting and a video at the hotel Friday evening, players dispersed to their rooms. Saturday morning would begin with an early breakfast because of the one o'clock kickoff. There would be no pep rally on the quad for this first game.

"I know I can't sleep this early," Willy said, sitting on the edge of the bed, eyeing the clock on the nightstand.

They each perused their three-ring binder of notes for a while, but the material had grown old. Neither of them had an appetite to study further, and Willy flipped on the television and began surfing channels. When the news came on, he stopped. ALERT. The graphics caught his attention.

Topping our news tonight, a missing Nashville man has the attention of police the anchor said. *After failing to arrive for his shift Sunday night at Plastics International, authorities were summoned to the home of supervisor Joe Daily. Fearing the worst, police gained entrance and were unable to locate anyone at the residence.*

Joey's eyes were wide and realizing his shock might be visible to Willy, he tried to remain calm and act natural. Then the screen shot broke to video of Glenn looking dapper in his Cardinals cap.

When Joe didn't show up Sunday, I knew somethin' was wrong. He didn't call in. Nobody's seen 'im. It's not like Joe. He wouldn't do this.

Then the scene shifted to video of Joe's home and immediately to video of what looked like a detective in a suit. The detective spoke next.

Joe Daily's vehicle was still in the drive, and upon searching we located items that would indicate he was not involved in a robbery. It appears he has simply vanished.

Joey thought about the uncashed check. He thought about his friends at the plant and how worried they must be and felt a pang of sadness for subjecting them to his decision. The television screen switched to a picture of Joe Daily and his name printed in bold letters to the side.

If anyone has any information on Joe Daily, the man pictured on the screen, police want you to contact them as soon as possible. If you have information, you can call our tip line on the screen or the number of the Nashville Metro Police, also pictured. Mr. Daily has now been entered as missing. All tips will be kept confidential.

It's football time here in Nashville, and the Commodores...

"Huh," Willy said. "Wonder what happened there?"

"No telling," Joey said. He suddenly felt tired and conspicuous even though his appearance had changed so much there was no resemblance, so he crawled up the bed, turned it down, and made himself comfortable. "Let's get some rest."

As the stadium filled on Saturday, players went through taping and their last minute preparations reviewing the Hilltoppers' team. Their quarterback was a fast, agile fifth-year senior who had led the team to its best finish in school history and a bowl win last year. What he lacked in passing expertise he made up for in everything else. The line returned intact. The defensive front looked to be the team's weakness, but if the Commodores got into a shootout the game might get away from them.

After warm-ups on the field, Michaels addressed the team. What the Commodores lacked in physical ability, they more than made up for in preparation and enthusiasm. And what stood out for Joey was the way the team had become a unit, even with their late additions who they had accepted and nurtured as one of their own. It gave Joey hope, albeit only a glimmer, and now with Al's help winning might indeed be reality.

The team's original kicker had recovered enough to perform on kickoffs and on the first play of the 'Dores' season he sent the ball into the end zone. Vandy stopped an off-tackle play to the right for no gain then stopped an option to the left. The quarterback's third down pass was high and the ensuing punt went out of bounds near the fifty, leaving Vandy in good field position.

But Vandy's offense didn't cooperate. With the quarterback in the shotgun on the first play, the center snapped the ball over his head for a ten yard loss. In a case of apparent first game nerves, Ronnie Couch ran into the halfback on the next play for another loss. On third and long, his first pass attempt went high, and it was time for Joey to make his first appearance in his first college game.

The snap was true, and Joey watched the defense peel away for the return. The rush was light. A large open spot spread to the right of the field, and had Joey decided to run he would have picked up the first down easily. He hesitated and then kicked. The punt was a beautiful, high spiral, like all his punts, and by the time it fell to Earth Vandy players waited to catch it. They did so at the one yard line, 64 yards away.

His position coach met him on the sideline with a high five, but Michaels was there as well.

"If they do that again, run for it. It was open," he said. Joey had been right. He had the green light should it happen again.

The Hilltoppers got out of trouble on the first play, executing the option that failed on the first drive. Then, their nimble quarterback eluded the rush and sprinted for 29 yards. After completing a long pass, they were across the fifty yard line. That's where they stalled and had to punt. Their kick went out of bounds at the ten.

It looked like Couch was going to have one of those days. He bobbled the snap when he pulled out too soon from center, and after falling on the ball he threw incompletions on the next two plays. Now, Joey would be punting from his own end zone. There would be no return this time. Almost certainly Western Kentucky would bring everyone, and from the looks of all the players revving up on the line that would be the case.

He waited for the snap. And the worst happened.

The snap looked good initially, but as it traveled back to Joey it was clear the ball would be high. It was. The ball kept climbing. Joey leaped, and got one hand on it, tipping it straight up in the air in a crazy wobble. When Joey caught it, he saw players bearing down on him from the right and left. He took one step and at the last moment spun right. The defender whizzed by in the air. Another came and he dodged left. Then, the defender originally flying in from the left jumped and Joey spun out of the way once more. He put his head down and ran, past the goal line, with two more players in hot pursuit.

Thinking back later, he had no idea why he did it. Maybe it was one of those situations that Al had told him would simply happen. Joey, in a split second, slammed on the brakes, and in that instant – as the defenders sensed he had stopped and stuttered – Joey accelerated to full speed once more. The defenders were suddenly behind him. Several other Hilltoppers scattered around the field in front of him, each closing, but now Joey's teammates were blocking.

Joey began to follow his own players, accelerating then running around packs of players. When he at last faced the lone return man, Joey planted and ran away from him and toward the end zone in the distance. Technically, Joey had executed a 94 yard run a touchdown, and a lead for Vandy.

He had no time to celebrate though. Vandy's kicker was once again hurting and could not kick extra points. Joey tacked on the extra point, and then kicked off.

The kick off went through the end zone for a touchback.

The first quarter ended at 7-0. And that's the way the first half ended after several fumbles and interceptions.

Willy, who had yet to get into the game, met Joey in the concourse.

"They couldn't touch you," he said, slapping Joey's number 99 on the back of his jersey.

"It was like slow motion," Joey said. He didn't add how good it felt either.

The second half was not like the first. Vandy began to get into their game. Their SEC size and speed began to wear down the Hilltoppers. If the Western Kentucky quarterback had not been in the game, the score would have been even worse. Vandy led 14-0 after three, only because the quarterback had scrambled for well over 100 yards and kept the Vanderbilt offense on the sidelines. Each time it seemed a punt was imminent he bobbed and weaved for a big gain. Finally, on the first play of the fourth quarter, he managed to elude everyone making the score 14-7.

Then Willy got into the game. If any play could have been labeled "Willy's Play", this was it. A simple end around, where Willy, flanked out to the right, ran full speed behind the quarterback and took a toss to race around to the left. Willy caught the pitch and sprinted far to the left. The field clogged. He stopped and reversed course, not an action the coaches wanted, but Willy's instinct had taken over. Willy gave ground and then cut the ball up, juked one man, hurdled another would-be tackler, and weaved his way all the way to pay dirt. 21-7.

Late in the fourth, Western Kentucky had the ball on their own thirty. One more stop and the game was history.

"Joey!" Michaels yelled. The defensive unit had assembled in front of their head coach before taking the field. "Go in at free safety. Stay about ten yards behind the middle linebackers. Everyone will do their job. Act like he's not there," he told them. "Joey, you are to watch the quarterback. Shadow him. He starts to run, he's yours. Watch us. We'll direct you each play."

Joey ran out with the team and to his spot.

"You got him," the team's middle linebacker and captain said, his eyes narrow slits. "Pop him if you get the chance."

The first play was a designed quarterback draw all the way. The quarterback took two steps back after the shotgun snap and bolted to the line looking for a hole. One of the guards had come straight for the linebacker and had him engaged as Joey darted around them. The linebacker on the left side of the line got tangled with another player, and Joey could see the qb's eyes, wild and wide, full of adrenalin. The quarterback made a half-hearted move to the right then lowered his shoulder in an attempt to run over Joey, who had other plans. Joey broke down and exploded into the quarterback and the ball. The ball carrier's head snapped back in the violent collision, his helmet flew backward, the ball seemed to sit suspended in mid-air. Joey, who never even fell to the ground reached out, collected it, and sprinted for his second score of the day.

The final was 28-7.

Joey made it to the locker room, and before anyone knew it two then three then four reporters had surrounded him at his locker.

"Joey, how did you like your first game?" one reporter said.

"It was fun, really fun," Joey said.

"You seem to be a big play machine," another prompted.

"I try to do what the coaches tell me."

Before another question could be asked, Michaels intervened and showed the reporters the door.

"I'm sorry," Michaels said. "We have a policy that freshmen don't talk to the media. I never saw this coming."

"That's good," Joey said. He was actually relieved. "Thanks, I didn't know what to do."

"You did fine. Enjoy this win. We've got work to do. You're going to be a busy guy."

He was busy. He was player of the week in the SEC.

Chapter 9

Life would never be the same for Willy or Joey, but they had no way of knowing how soon that would happen. It started at the pizzeria, their new favorite hangout, after the game. The owner, George, a Greek man with Elvis hair, not exactly Italian in either respect, smiled in recognition as they entered.

"Hello, you boys again," he said. "I give you table by the TV, yeah?"

"Thanks, George," Willy said. "Been busy?"

"Ah, yes, we very busy after the game. Everybody happy. You see the game?"

"We saw it," Willy said, glancing at Joey as the man walked away.

"I like that guy," Joey said.

"He remembered us, too."

"Willy, I'm amazed. You remembered his name."

"There's a lot more of us coming in here. We're only two people."

"But you got his name. He only knew us by sight."

"Joey, I've always found it's best to remember people's names. Everyone likes that. Makes them feel special."

A waitress came by and took their order, a large pizza, two Cokes. She still had her hands full with the after game crowd, and she bustled away back to the kitchen after scribbling on her pad. The television was tuned to football highlights which captured Willy and Joey's attention. In a few minutes, after highlights of the Big Orange, they saw Joey taking a snap as he stood in his own end zone. Willy hit Joey on the shoulder.

What about highlights from none other than Vanderbilt where stars are in the making. Unknown, walk-on freshmen at that. Joey Goodman takes the snap. Punt's gonna' be blocked, but no, wooop, he spins, turns, and now he's off to the races.

Watch him go. When was the last time Vandy had that kind of speed. He kicks extra points too, folks. Now let's see the other freshman. Willy Jackson, taking the pitch, he reverses field, and he's gone too.

"We're famous," Willy said, his smile as wide as the ocean.

As Willy sprinted down the field, the crowd in the restaurant, noticing the highlights of the game, began to yell and cheer. When he got to the end zone, the crowd erupted.

But maybe the hit of the day. He's on defense this time. Joey Goodman. Ouch!

Joey watched the helmet fly off and sat stunned as he saw himself catching the ball and racing away. The crowd in the restaurant let out a groan and then a whoop of excitement.

All the way to the end zone. He scores again. Vandy goes on to win 28-7. Hey freshman, what is it like to play in the SEC?

Then Joey saw his face as the short interview began. His eyes darted around the crowded restaurant, wondering if anyone would recognize him. He looked down to the table and picked up a menu, putting it in front of his face.

"Come on, Joey. You can't do that the whole time we're here. Might as well get used to it," Willie said as he pushed the table back and stood. "Joey Goodman, ladies and gentlemen!" he screamed pointing down to his friend.

The restaurant erupted with all eyes on him now. Joey waved and looked down again, but he did manage a smile.

By the time they had finished their pizza, dozens of people had asked for autographs. The co-eds at a table near theirs giggled and glanced at them throughout. Even though it wasn't an altogether unpleasant experience, Joey was quite uncomfortable. He wanted to be back in the privacy of his dorm room, maybe playing pool, and joking around with the guys as he had always done at the plant. In his mind he remained a man, past his prime, past middle age, not looking for the company of young women.

The next day, as they walked over to the field house for film study, several students noticed them and said "Good game". They wouldn't be bombarded again until they entered their classes, but throughout the week, especially after Joey was recognized as Player of the Week in the SEC, the attention grew. And by the time Friday's pep rally for the Austin Peay game began, signs with Joey's name had begun to appear. Willy's recognition was a close second. And with another pushover team, this one from Nashville as well, it seemed fans had decided to enjoy this ride as long as they could.

Other than having a strong-armed quarterback, Austin Peay was weak. Even though Vandy's line was small by SEC standards, the Commodores cruised from the very beginning, so much so Joey never even had to punt. The team had grown in leaps and bounds between their first and second game. Willy caught four passes, one of them only four yards past the line of scrimmage that he took eighty yards for a score. Joey had the chance to learn his safety position, all with the knowledge that his opponent did not have the talent or expertise to exploit his inexperience. He broke up the only pass that came in his direction. More importantly though, Michaels didn't have to show any of his blitz packages and that included all the ones designed to use Joey's speed. Joey did kick eight extra points in the 56-0 shellacking.

Next week would tell the tale though. The team would be playing on the road for the first time against Ole Miss. Who would have thought both teams would be 2-0 entering the game? And who would have thought that Michaels and his coaching staff still had more tricks up their sleeve and those tricks included a high power speedster named Joey Goodman?

Chapter 10

Each of the Vandy players watched their own DVD of "highlights", plays that were good, those that could be improved, and of course some that were missed assignments or mismatches. Each player had been graded on yesterday's performance already. There would be few mismatches in Vandy's favor this week playing Ole Miss.

After signing four five-star players two years ago and two last year, this team had talent. Considering how much the

Rebels had developed their four stars, beating them would be a real task. And now, the lights in the major film room dimmed, and Michaels began to break down what made the Ole Miss offense tick. He mentioned their best players by number, and then he explained several of their alignments. Most of the players, including Willy and Joey, took notes.

Then Michaels went to the defensive side of the ball. The Rebels front four, and their subs as well, not only did their assignments but also overwhelmed their opponents. They were quick, and they were big.

When the units dispersed, Michaels retained Joey and the team's two captains.

"I wanted to discuss some things with you guys. Ronnie, you in particular. First, we're getting beat, and I mean beat bad, at tackle. We've got guys as slow as the ones we played this week, running by those guys. We don't have more speed and size to insert in those spots, so we're going to have to get their big, fast tackles to over-commit and get out of position.

"And, this is why I wanted to talk with all three of you, we're going to have to try and get Joey the ball. I see him as being capable of doing things with the ball. Ronnie, we're going to put him in the backfield, sometimes getting the snap directly. We'll flank you out wide sometimes. Sometimes you may come out. You are our captain, and you've done well. We have to do what we can though to score points."

The senior quarterback nodded and rolled the idea around before he said, "I want to win, coach. Let's do it."

"Mark," the coach continued, "we're also going to put Joey back deep on kickoffs, with you. We may even have him return some punts."

Dennison agreed as well.

They would begin working tomorrow. Joey would have to be ready if Vandy had any hope of beating Ole Miss.

As Joey and Willy left the long meeting and walked through the campus, the weight of the conversations settled over them. The planning had been serious, but more playing time had come their way. Finally, Willy said what was on both of their minds, and it revealed what they really thought.

"We're starting!" Willy yelled and immediately looked around to make certain none of the other players were close.

Joey smiled, but it was a hollow feeling in one sense. He knew this would eventually be his destiny. Would Vandy win every game, or would he simply be the shining star? That was where he wasn't as certain. Joey wondered if Willy might have met Al, or someone like him, at some point. He didn't think so, but then again it was easy to imagine while watching Willy play. But the uneasy feeling, the feeling that he was doing something wrong – something so very fundamentally wrong that it was a sin in itself- gnawed at his gut.

Joey saw Al, sitting on the steps of Fowler Hall, leaning back enjoying the evening.

"Willy, I need to go speak to this gentleman."

Willy stopped walking, looked across to the steps where Al sat, and then turned back to his friend.

"Okay. Alright, man, I'll see you back."

Al stood and stepped down to greet Joey. They shook hands.

"Are you getting taller, Joey?"

He hadn't considered the prospect that at 19 years old he might still be growing, but it was fine by him. Joey had always wanted to be six feet tall. For a moment, a fleeting second, he returned to his youth and what it was like to grow and look forward to what he might become as an adult. It was the first time in years he had felt this way, and in the same instant he became young again. He didn't just look young and feel a more youthful body. He actually had returned to his youth with an altogether different outlook on the way things were inside his earthly body.

"I might be, Al."

"How is college life?" Al asked.

"Easier than I imagined. My former degree is helping me write all these assignments and papers. I guess I still have it."

"That you do, my boy. I've not helped you there in the least."

"You were right. I can play. I don't even think about it, and it happens."

"It's great isn't it? You don't have to wait all one-hundred days, you know."

Somehow, Joey did know that. But there was more. He had rehearsed this time, now, and he decided it was time to play the game. His confidence, along with his youthful body, had begun to mature as well.

"There's more. I know it." Joey stopped short. He still wondered if Al could possibly read his thoughts. He thought not and had considered that even though there was much Al could do it was possible he was shrewd and cunning, a keen observer of facial expressions and body language. Knowing much about someone made guessing all that much easier. Maybe that's how Al had known to push his buttons about Michelle.

"There's almost anything you want," Al said. He smiled again and rocked back on his feet.

"If I had almost everything I wanted, there's almost no end to what I might do."

"You say it, Joey. I'd venture to say most anything is possible."

"Let's leave it at that then for now," Joey said. He suddenly felt as though some of the cards had shifted in his favor. He might have a bit of the upper hand.

"One hundred days, Joey. Have you counted it up?"

He had considered it, yes. Near the end of the season and the SEC Championship game. He had to buy some time after that, and he thought he might know how to do that. But was it possible to beat the devil at his own game?

"I might have," Joey said. "I'll see you around."

"One hundred days," Al said to Joey's back as the young man walked away. "One hundred days. And not a second more."

Joey entered the dorm and bounded up the stairs and into the hallway of the second floor.

"Wa-wa-wa-wa-wait!" someone screamed.

Guys stood in each of the doorways, their heads peering out into the hall. Near the midway point of the hall, a band of toilet paper stretched across and on the other end several students stood behind Downtown Kevin Brown and another student, Dante Stillworth, a stout and muscular sophomore who looked like a professional boxer. Dante acted like one as well.

"We're going to race," Downtown said from the other end about thirty yards away.

Willy stood in one of the open doors. He still had not made it to his room. The amusing sight made him smile.

"Downtown said he was pretty fast for a fat man. He's racing Dante," Willy said.

"Why didn't they go run in the field?" Joey asked. The participants had begun to set up their start once more.

"Downtown said he couldn't run that far. He said he was quick, not fast at the top end."

"SET!" the starter yelled behind them.

"GO!"

There was a rumbling. Downtown almost got out in front of Dante, and he would have never let the other racer pass if that had happened. As it was they ran stride for stride. Ten yards, then twenty, roaring down the hall. As they passed each door, heads went inside and then back out at once to watch the race. The cheers were deafening. It seemed as though the floor would collapse.

Dante nipped him at the finish.

Downtown crumpled in a gargantuan heap in the floor.

"He IS fast for fat man!" Dante roared, laughing hard and catching his breath.

Downtown finally arose and strolled back into his room. Joey and Willy stood amazed. He was fast, and so big.

"You know what I'm thinking," Joey said to Willy.

Downtown's roommate walked by on his way to check on Downtown.

"Greer," Willy said as one of the students passed, "did he ever play football?"

"No, man," Greer answered. "His brother said he went out his sophomore year and he thought he hurt a guy. He only played about three days."

"He's so big," Joey said. They were walking toward Downtown's room.

"He set Marion County's lifting records too in the off-season. He only worked out about two weeks. He's a big teddy bear."

Downtown was sprawled on the bed, his arms and legs hanging off each side, a scene that looked like someone had shot a grizzly bear.

"I was telling them what your brother told me," Greer said.

Downtown didn't move. If his chest had not been rising and falling it might have been easy to mistake him for being dead.

Willy grabbed Downtown's leg and shook him. "You're big and fast."

"My brother's bigger than I am," Downtown said still motionless. "Funny. He was about five-ten his freshman year, and he ate nothing but peanut butter. He was six-five by the start of his sophomore year."

"When you catch your breath, come to my room," Willy told him. He and Joey walked out and down the hall. "We've got to get that guy to come out."

Joey and Willy sat in the room and waited for Downtown. Willy leaned back, apparently tired from the day's classroom work and sore from yesterday's game. Joey felt surprisingly energetic. He had found that he needed little sleep and his recovery time was off the charts. In all fairness though, he had played little in the Austin Peay game.

"Who was that guy?" Willy asked, his eyes still closed as he leaned back.

"What guy?"

"The guy you were talking to."

"That guy? Oh, my uncle. He stops by. He makes sure I'm doing okay. He kind of started looking after me after dad died." Joey wondered if the lying would ever come more easily, even though this fib hadn't been too difficult.

"Okay. Just worried about you, you know. There's boosters and agents. So many ways to get into trouble, you know?"

"I know. Thanks Willy."

The conversation was unproductive with Downtown, but he promised to consider going to speak to Michaels. Downtown was having altogether too much fun to be bogged down with practice. He did have an adventuresome soul though, or so it seemed. Willy was persuasive as well. He seemed to have a way of making others feel almost bad if they didn't come around to his way of thinking no matter what the topic. His intentions seemed honorable and worthy.

Workouts the week of the Ole Miss game were hard up until Wednesday. Every player seemed to be lifting the intensity. Drills were vigorous as well. But most of the work on the field seemed to be mental. By the end of practice Wednesday, the coaching staff had other concerns as well. The weather was turning nasty. A hurricane had bounced up through the gulf and looked as though it would crash through Biloxi and take a path through Mississippi. Saturday would be, at best, wet and blustery.

On Thursday Downtown accompanied Willy and Joey to see Michaels. Kevin would begin working with the team the following week. But for now, the team would leave on Friday morning and travel to Oxford for their first SEC game where the chase for a title would begin. The game would likely make or break one of the teams.

Chapter 11

The rain began Thursday night, but not with a gentle patter in the dark September sky but rather with a clap of thunder after the wind had begun to whistle through the window creases in the dorm. Joey leaned back in a chair, light over his shoulder with a text book now in his lap, and watched the water spray and streak down his window overlooking the courtyard. Tyler's door opened, and the young man strode barefoot in a stupor into the common area. He wore sweat pants and a gray t-shirt with the word "Vandy" across the front. Joey hadn't seen his face in two weeks.

"The hurricane got here," Tyler said.

"I don't think this is really Sally yet." Joey closed his book and sat up.

"The wind," Tyler began again, "will we have a tornado? Have you watched the weather?"

In fact, Joey hadn't watched the weather. He only knew that instead of a short flight to Oxford the team would leave on buses tomorrow morning. The storm was supposed to pass Oxford early Saturday before the game, leaving behind only rain and wind, not the twisting action of what would be a tropical depression. For now, Ole Miss braced to be pounded by the hurricane.

"I haven't watched the weather. I think we're fine though."

Instead of padding back to his room, Tyler turned and sat in a chair facing Joey. He rubbed his eyes and seemed to be thinking.

"Joey, how do you do this?" he asked.

Joey wasn't sure exactly what Tyler was asking and he answered with the expression on his face.

"I mean, how do you go to class, study, play football, and hang out with the guys. You never sleep."

"I sleep," Joey said. He sat up straighter. "I mean, I don't sleep much. I haven't slept much in years." He caught himself when he realized what he had spoken. What could years be for a nineteen-year-old who was really fifty?

"I want to be a real college student. I can't fail though. My dad would kill me. I can't go make friends and run around. What would they say if I had to come back and study?"

"Tyler, most students here say that. We all have to study. They would understand. More than likely they would try to convince you to discontinue doing whatever you're doing at the moment, but they would understand."

"You probably think I'm a freak."

"No. No, I don't. Why would you say that?"

"Because I'm never out of my room except to go to class." Tyler looked away into the small kitchen.

"I don't judge you. Truth be told, I don't think others judge you as much as you think. They're too busy worrying about being judged." Joey laughed eliciting the same from Tyler.

Joey stood and looked out the window as the rain cascaded through the street lights in sheets that swept against the side of the building and blotted out all the details of the courtyard. The weather was going to make the game even more interesting. How could he run and utilize his speed in this?

"I'm going back to bed," Tyler said.

Joey turned back around. He felt as though he needed to say more to his roommate, but he couldn't decide what.

"Okay, good night. Don't worry about the storm. I'll wake you if it gets bad."

Tyler stepped toward his room and stopped. "Joey, if you're gone before I get up, good luck in the game. I'll be watching."

"Thanks."

"You're wise beyond your years," Tyler said. "I could tell from the first time I met you."

The buses pulled out of the parking lot at eight a.m. on the button, and rain buffeted the windows and the wind rocked the team back and forth throughout the four hour ride to Oxford. The team did a walk through indoors that evening, all under the watchful eye of the commentators for the SEC game of the week who sat in folding chairs on the sideline. That night Sally, barely downgraded from a hurricane, roared through town.

The rain continued under dark gray skies throughout breakfast, and by the time the team came out of the dressing room to begin warm-ups a steady downpour and intermittent wind gusts were all that remained. The turf held remarkably well, and Joey found that he had little difficulty cutting or planting. He seemed to be as fast as ever. By the time the Ole Miss band finished the "National Anthem", a raucous crowd in the stadium full to capacity ignored the rain and waited to learn which team would walk out of the stadium 3-0.

Even though the wind was in his face, Joey put the opening kickoff deep into the end zone. The Rebels began to march at once, slipping a pass to a halfback on the far side of the field away from Joey. Then, the quarterback scrambled for fifteen yards before Joey slammed him to the ground. A counter play for ten more. Another pass away from Joey. Then a reverse to the five. It took Ole Miss three more plays, but they punched the ball into the end zone for a 7-0 lead.

All of Michaels' hopes of not using Joey to a great extent evaporated on the Commodores first possession. Three insignificant plays for no gain and a Joey Goodman punt inside the twenty. Ole Miss repeated their first drive and made the score 14-0, all with plays designed to steer clear as far as possible from Joey.

On Vandy's second drive, Joey didn't get a chance to make an impact either. With Joey split out wide, Couch muffed another snap and the ball got kicked around all the way to the end zone where the Rebels recovered it to make the score 21-0. The rain continued. It looked to be a gloomy day for Vandy all the way around. Every Ole Miss' supporter was breathing a sigh of relief, and most certainly the announcers had been convinced that Vanderbilt's fast start to the season was more a mirage than an oasis.

Vanderbilt's spirits were low and heads hung as they came off the field.

"Get your heads up!" Michaels yelled. "It's only over if you think it is. Joey! Run the kick back!"

Vanderbilt's fortunes were about to change.

The Ole Miss kicker tried to pooch the ball to the sideline and instead the wind carried it all the way back to Joey on the goal line. Bloated raindrops fell in his eyes as he waited and by the time he caught it two Rebel defenders were bearing down on him. He sidestepped one and spun away from the second. Then he saw the wall, wide open on the far side of the field as if the Red Sea had parted. Ten, twenty, thirty yard line before one defender broke through, and Joey sidestepped and put his head down. Forty, fifty, forty, no one in sight. Touchdown Vandy. Joey's extra point made the score 21-7.

The rain fell harder. Joey topped the ball on the kickoff bouncing it high, and as he ran beneath it he leveled the first Ole Miss player in his way. When it bounced again, Joey caught it in stride, eluded one man and outran everyone to the end zone again. Kick. 21-14. Now the fans had a ballgame as the wind and rain came harder.

Joey's next kickoff was a line drive that careened off a player on the front line and all the way back to Vandy who fell on it. Vandy began to drive at once. Couch took the snap and ran a quarterback sneak surprising everyone and good for ten yards inside Ole Miss territory. Then, Joey went in motion and intercepted the shotgun snap, streaked around the end, made a man miss and scored again. After the kick, the game was tied.

The Vandy defense held on long enough for the Rebels to miss a field goal, now into the wind, and the teams were still knotted at the end of three quarters. The mood on the sideline was one of relief; a reprieve had been granted, and it seemed as though Vandy now believed they could win the game.

The fourth quarter was never close. The Rebels came back onto the field for the kickoff as if the rain and wind buffeted only them and as if they had no desire to be playing at all. Joey ran back a punt, picked a pass for a touchdown on the next play, and then returned another punt for a touchdown. He seemed to be everywhere. He wanted the ball every play. If he was on defense he often made the tackle. Joey scored on one more play from the shotgun giving him seven td's and seven extra points on the day. Willie caught a screen and went the distance late in the game, and the final score was 56-21.

Vandy was 3-0, and Joey Goodman would become a household name by the end of the week.

Chapter 12

After a catered meal and showers, the Vanderbilt buses got out of town sandwiched in between two Tennessee State Trooper cruisers. The rain continued, but it didn't seem that bad going back, especially for Joey. The players, who had been so quiet on the trip into town on Friday, sang, laughed, and joked. By 9:30 they entered the parking lot of the field house and most everyone's jaw dropped.

Thousands of people stood in the rain, some under umbrellas, many drenched and jumping up and down, children and adults waving and carrying wilting poster board signs. Players lowered windows and waved and yelled. Lines of people followed the parking buses. Car horns blared. The fans cheered as the players climbed out and began collecting bags.

Students slapped Joey on the back and children held pens and items to autograph. He signed a few and tried to get in out of the rain. Encouragement, thanks, all manner of praise. Vandy was 3-0. Then the girls appeared. They found Joey. More than one gave him a phone number. He followed Willy trying to escape graciously, but a part of him wanted to stay, to celebrate, and to bask in the glow of the win. He felt invigorated.

The dorm was a madhouse. Someone played a beat on what sounded like a steel garbage can. Others chanted. Dante formed a conga line surrounding their two heroes. Joey and Willy ducked into Downtown's room and found him sprawling not on the bed but the floor.

"What's the matter with you? Did you see the game?" Willy asked him before smacking his large rear end.

Downtown didn't move and only muttered, "Someone shoot me."

"Why, Downtown?" Joey asked.

"My brother is trying to kill me. We worked out, in the rain, on the field, for two hours. Up and down steps. Pushups and sit-ups. Put me out of my misery."

Joey left Willy to continue the celebration and drug his bag into his room. Tyler, sitting at the table, looked up from his reading.

"Hey, Tyler."

"You, you did great," Tyler said. He pushed his glasses up on his nose.

"Thanks. Really. You watched?"

"I did. I can hardly believe it."

"Well join the club," Joey said finally closing the door behind him.

"They took the downstairs phone off the hook. You've been getting about a million calls. They brought some messages up here before they finally gave up. I slid them under your door."

Joey opened the door, picked up the small stack of papers, and examined a few. Many of them were from girls. Some only numbers. He was glad he didn't have a cell phone.

"I'm just going to sit here and unwind. You care if I turn on the TV?"

"No, go ahead."

Joey started to watch Sports Center. He knew he'd be on there, and maybe he see how he looked in action. Instead, he flipped around the channels, growing somewhat numb. What had he done today? How could he have scored all those touchdowns? But instead of feeling guilty, he began to have the feeling he wanted to go out and celebrate. He wanted to see what the limelight was all about. But upon realizing what he was considering, the sensation startled him.

He found the ten o'clock local news coming on and stopped.

The mystery of the disappearance of Joe Daily continues in Nashville the anchor said. *Neighbors saw a suspicious vehicle and two unknown men on the last day Daily was seen, and now investigators are probing whether he might have been involved in questionable dealings.*

Mr. Johnson, Mr. Daily's neighbor, says that he could never imagine Joe Daily being involved in anything illegal. He's a good, hardworking man. We're worried sick that something bad has happened to 'im. *For now, the investigation continues.*

Joey was jolted back to reality.

A detective was interviewed and explained that nothing in the case added up. Witnesses had seen strange men on the day of the disappearance. What had Joe Daily been up to? Joey heard a voice inside his head say *You would never believe it.*

The door flew open, and Downtown's humongous head peered inside.

"We're going to The Club to throw darts. Wanna go with us?"

Joey thought about it for a moment. He wasn't tired in the least, and there was probably no hope of sleeping anytime soon. He did want to go.

"Tyler, you want to go with us?" Joey asked.

"No, you go ahead. I'm going to knock out," Tyler said. He turned his attention to the television.

"You should go with us. Come on. It'll be fun."

"No, really. You go on."

For a moment Joey considered staying behind and maybe sitting around with his roommate. Maybe he could get to know him a little bit or at least break the tension that seemed to hang around them at all times. At the same time, something else tugged at him.

"Let's do it," Joey said.

There were eight of them. Downtown, who was like a large child bouncing against the other guys and making one silly observation after another, had made a miraculous recovery. Willy had declined the invitation to go with them, Joey thought probably due to his past troubles that seemed to flank his every move.

The Club catered to the young college crowd not old enough to even drink yet in Tennessee and was filled with that very crowd. The darkness swallowed them when they entered, and they stood in the doorway scanning the tables and letting their eyes adjust.

"Chicks. Two o'clock. Throwing darts. Come on, Joey," Downtown said.

"I dunno," Joey replied.

"Come on. Girls," Downtown said pushing him in that direction. "You know you want to."

"Kevin, I don't know. Really-"

"I came out for the football team. It's the least you could do."

"You came out for Willy, and your brother. You go talk 'em up."

"They won't give me the time of day," Kevin said. "I need a wingman of your stature."

Downtown prodded and pushed until they stood directly behind the girls. One of them, a little blonde wearing tight jeans and a loose halter top, stood with her hand on her hip and seemed to be demonstrating a cheer move for her friend, a brunette wearing a small skirt. Downtown was right. They probably wouldn't give them the time of day. Joey realized he was thinking like Joe Daily. They might not give Downtown the time of day, but they probably would Joey.

What Downtown lacked in sex appeal, he made up for in charisma and charm.

"Hello, ladies," he began. "I see we have a fine game of darts taking place at this board."

"Yes, we do," the brunette said glancing back at Downtown for one quick second. The blonde didn't even acknowledge them.

"We could make this a foursome," Kevin continued. He was persistent; you had to give him that.

"We're kind of with those guys over there," brunette said again. She motioned to a table nearby, and sure enough Downtown and Joey's arrival had drawn the attention of four tanned and preppy young men. Their eyes burned into the conversation at the dart board.

It was time to go nuclear.

"Ladies, I hate to bother you, but I'd like for you to meet someone."

Brunette turned and gave Downtown a look of disdain. She was well versed in rejecting advances from men not on the upper echelon of alpha. She let out an audible sigh. Blonde continued averting her eyes from the conversation.

"I'd like for you to meet Joey Goodman."

The girls turned to Joey and stopped. Now this had not been discussed in their pre-approved game plan. They seemed to size him up.

"Hi girls," Joey said. He wondered if the words had sounded out loud as strange and creepy as they sounded inside his head.

"Hi Joey," brunette said. She smiled. Apparently the words had not sounded creepy.

"You go to Vanderbilt?" blonde asked.

"I do. I'm a freshman."

"He plays football," Kevin continued. The brunette was definitely into Joey, and it appeared as if that would leave the blonde. Kevin seemed to be fine with that. But more work had to be done. "If you saw the game today, he beat Ole Miss."

"Kevin, really-"

"No, he did. He really did. How many touchdowns?"

"I think seven."

"Seven touchdowns. He's great."

The girls had not seen the game. They did seem impressed though, and in a turn of events that had never happened to Joey in real life, brunette reached out and stroked his right bicep with her index finger as she locked onto his eyes.

The sensation was beyond electric. A shiver went up Joey's spine.

"Are these guys bothering you?" asked one of the young men from the table. The other three stood behind him.

"Kevin, we're fine," brunette said to him. *How many guys at Vanderbilt were named Kevin?*

"'Cause they look like they're bothering you," the new Kevin continued.

"This is Joey Goodman," she said.

"And Kevin," Downtown said, "Kevin Brown." The big man looked to the blonde who half smiled and looked away. This wingman thing might not be going according to plan after all.

"Wait. Joey? Joey Goodman?" the new Kevin asked. Joey nodded. "Good God. I saw you today. This is the guy."

The others knew already and had broken into grins.

"I can't believe it. You ran all over them. You're going to win the Heisman."

"Well-"

"No, I'm serious. I've never seen anyone play like you," new Kevin continued. He turned Joey around, and now the brunette lost her smile and grasped Joey's arm a bit harder and spun him back toward her. The young man twisted Joey back around and continued. "I have to know. Do you plan a move when you see these guys coming, or does it just happen?"

"Joey, we can-" brunette began and new Kevin cut her off once more.

"You make these moves-"

"I don't think much, I-" Joey said, and then brunette spun him back to her more forcefully. The tug of war was flattering but Joey was beginning to grow disoriented.

That's when *she* stepped between them.

She didn't look like a normal co-ed. She was a woman. Dressed to kill. And if it could be put into words, she looked dangerous. The conversation stopped altogether, and a quiet settled over the group. Even Downtown retreated.

"Hi, Joey. I'm Luan." She extended her hand, fingers slightly down and Joey took it. The handshake was not firm, it was feminine. And warm. Her perfume overwhelmed all the other smells in the room and massaged Joey's senses. Her hand was so, so, so soft. He couldn't look away from her eyes, blue and radiant as if they had starlight beams extending from the center in a mesmerizing, and hypnotic glow.

"Hi," Joey said. "I'm-"

Joey started to say his name and realized that Luan had already spoken it. He couldn't take his eyes off her. Instead, he muttered, "I'm glad to meet you."

Luan pulled Joey away from the crowd and waved goodbye to the group as she led him like a puppy on a leash. Still holding his hand she led him across the club, cutting through the dance floor, and then to a dark corner where a table sat. She eased him into a high swivel-chair, and instead of sitting in the adjacent seat, she pushed up against him. She was soft and warm, and her smell engulfed him in something resembling the pheromones of a queen bee.

"Kids these days," she said and laughed, leaning her head back exposing her soft neck, the taut sinewy lines of feline muscle rising to her beautiful face, her pouty lips, and round, even teeth.

"Um, you must have seen the game."

"I see every game, Joey. I'm the head cheerleader."

"Oh, that's good. I can see that. I mean-"

"I know what you mean," she said. Still she looked him in the eye. She hadn't looked away since she intercepted him. "I like the strong, shy type. You've got something though. You get my motor running."

"Really?" Joey was reeling. He looked around the dance floor, but Luan turned his face back to her.

"Really."

This was new territory for Joey. Part of him wanted to slink away, to become Joe Daily again, to go back to the easy existence and a reality that he had grown familiar with over the last fifty years. Another part of him, the part that was winning right at the moment, wanted to stay. Forever.

"Got a girl, Joey?"

"I had a girl. I don't anymore," Joey said. For him, the spell was broken. The memories that had been pushed down into his depths rose up once more. His existence, though altered now, could never be changed. "I-"

"I don't have a guy either, Joey." Luan moved back a bit, and in the same motion she swiveled beside him. "You have such big shoulders."

Luan placed each hand on a shoulder and squeezed. The feeling was something approaching heaven.

"I have a busy day tomorrow, Luan. Can we talk sometime?"

Joey intended the comment to disrupt Luan's seduction, but there was enough testosterone coursing through his veins he was determined not to sever all lifelines.

"I have an apartment," she said, mashing her ample bosom against his back. "All by my lonesome."

So coy, so demure now.

"I'll see you then," Joey said. He stepped forward to escape. "I mean, I'll see you around. We'll talk."

"We will, Joey. I hope we will. I'd really like that."

Einstein must have been correct, because when Joey managed to drag Downtown away and back to the dorm the clock in his room said 3:00 proving time was relative. Joey slept as soon as he fell into bed and when he woke, he ate and then began the walk to the field house at almost noon. The now deserted campus sat recovering from last night's win. The rain had stopped and blue skies bathed the drying buildings and trees, still green awaiting the arrival of fall.

"Joey."

Joey saw Al, sitting on a bench, and he went to him. Joey waved but said nothing.

"Nice game. What will happen to this campus if you beat somebody *really* good?"

"I hope we find out."

"Keep playing the way you are and I'd say it's a certainty we'll find out." Al began to walk with Joey toward the field house. "Now things begin to get *really* crazy.

"What do you mean?"

"I mean, when people sense a star is born, they want a piece of the action. You're about to have more fun than you ever dreamed of having."

Joey wondered what that might entail. His idea of fun had been sitting at home watching a movie with Michelle. Playing Canasta on the kitchen table. Maybe walking in the park and watching fireworks on the Fourth of July. Hardly what Al could consider fun he was certain.

"Joey. Joey Goodman." The voice came from behind them. A man approached in a nice suit and shoes that clicked as he ran toward them. He carried a briefcase.

"Yes?"

"I'm Lenny Kniles. I'm a talent agent. I want to give you my card, and-"

Al intercepted the card and slipped it in his shirt pocket in one motion while at the same time stepping in between Joey and the agent.

"Lenny. Why don't you give him a call at the end of the season?"

"I-"

"You think he's a hot commodity now, wait until the end of the season. He'll be so hot, he'll have everyone howling all around him."

Lenny said nothing for a moment and when he began to speak again, Al lifted his finger and shooed him away, sending the man walking backward as if he was nothing more than a toy boat on a tranquil pond.

"Weird," Joey said.

"Not at all," Al said walking once more beside Joey. "Happens all the time. You just have to know the right people, my boy. Have fun. I'll see you around."

Joey stopped outside the field house and watched Al walk away whistling.

Chapter 13

Vandy was home again, this week against Northwestern, billed as a battle of brains. And, of course, ESPN was even carrying the game because of Joey Goodman. Excitement was building to a fever pitch with the prospect of the Commodores having a 4-0 record, which would be only the fourth time that had happened since 1950.

On Monday Vandy had also discovered that practices would have to be restricted somehow. The news media was everywhere, in the stands, on the sidelines, one reporter even walked out behind the huddle and tried to take a picture over Joey's shoulder.

The usually mild mannered Michaels erupted in a string of profanity that was so out of character several players laughed. After practice Michaels even chuckled at the outburst himself, causing his neck and face to glow in a soft pink hue and his eyes to water.

But the most pleasurable outcome of the winning streak was a positive difference in the attitude of the team. At Vanderbilt there is no shortage of players who believe in teamwork and who work hard in attempting to make that happen. That is the nature of a school with high academic standards and rigor. But the attitude of the team had begun to morph into intensity, accountability, and a level of play that could only be credited to having won. It was the chemistry and the intangible that those who watch games recognize and witness in champion teams.

If Northwestern was indeed as inferior as most pundits believed, no one would have surmised Vandy's players thought so after witnessing practices.

During the week, Joey thought about Luan several times a day. He tried to remember each of her features and pondered on the matter much more than he probably should have. Unlike a flower, plucked from its stem and more beautiful than an imitation because of its almost imperceptible and yet somehow known flaws and still exquisitely wonderful, Luan seemed to be unblemished and without defect. How she could have honed her seductive talents when her reward and prizes were to be had so easily was a mystery for Joey.

But when he didn't locate Luan on campus by Wednesday, he accepted the satisfaction that he would see her cheering on the sidelines Saturday.

In one sense the game was anticlimactic. In another, the game was incredible. If he wasn't a superstar already, Joey cemented that notion against Northwestern. He returned the opening kickoff 100 yards for a touchdown. He got a pick-six his first series on defense. He returned a punt for a touchdown on the next. Willy caught a screen pass, got a devastating pancake block from Joey and went the distance for a score. Joey ran a play from the shotgun eighty yards for an offensive score, then scored on a screen pass himself. Five more touchdowns. The game got out of hand so quickly, Joey didn't even play in the second half.

It appeared for a while that Downtown might get into the game, but the coaches weren't certain he was ready. His brother did play defense on the last series and even made a tackle.

During the second half, Joey finally spotted Luan. Several times he looked her way but she never gave him a glance, at least he didn't see it if she did. He decided to go to

The Club again tonight in the hope she would make an appearance.

Sports Center ran the highlights throughout the evening and late into the night on the recap show. Joey now led the nation in scoring and all-purpose yards. Vandy was almost a lock to enter the top 25 in the polls. And, if Vandy could possibly beat their next opponent, on the road in Columbia at #15 South Carolina, there was no telling how high the Commodores might rank. Vandy had not been 5-0 since 1943.

Joey returned from the late game well after midnight, managed to elude his entourage of dorm mates, and raced inside so as to shower and go out. Tyler had gone home for the weekend, and it didn't matter tonight if he went out alone. In fact, he planned to do just that. An unknown force, if Luan could be called that, beckoned, calling him to The Club. Joe, the old man, was gone. In his place was Joey Goodman, and that man had no time to waste.

As he picked one last time at his hair, he heard three solid raps on his door. Willy.

"Can I come in?" Willy asked.

"Sure," Joey said. He turned around and went back for one last look in the mirror and then began brushing his teeth once more.

Willy, in sweats and a t-shirt, sat on the couch and leaned back, watching Joey. He said nothing for a moment.

"Where you headed?" he asked finally.

"I'm going to The Club, Willy. You ought to come with me."

"No, no I shouldn't. I told you I'm not going down that path again."

"Willy. It's practically on campus," Joey said. He sat down on the couch near Willy and turned to face him. "It's safe. No drinking either."

"Who is she?"

"Who is who?"

"You know what I'm asking. Who is she?"

Joey stood and walked into the kitchen, got a bottle of water, and with it motioned at Willy to ask if he wanted one as well. Willy shook his head as he stared at his friend.

"Her name is Luan. She's gorgeous." Joey walked back and sat beside Willy once more.

"It's almost two, Joey."

"Willy, she has this vein in her forearm," Joey said. "Her skin is tan, but you can actually see her heartbeat in that little vein. She smells wonderful as well." Joey smiled and sipped as he continued smiling.

"You're going to The Club to see a woman's pulse."

"You put it that way, I sound like a vampire. I think I want to get out there again, you know, meet the girls. Willy, the girls watch the games. They see us on TV. I know they saw you today. You had two scores. They flock around like a bunch of hungry pigeons."

"Man, this isn't you."

"What do you mean this isn't me? I'm me. I like the ladies. And I know you like them too."

"And it got me in trouble."

"This isn't Beale Street. The odds of that happening again have to be astronomical."

"If I don't go out the odds are zero. You're a marked man and you don't even know it."

Something in the statement rocked Joey, but instead of even considering the point he shook his head, as if to clear the idea from his mind, and then stood once more and stepped toward the door.

"You can't live your life running away. You can't keep doing it, Willy. It's not healthy. Life's short. We don't have long. I mean, we're not going to be young forever."

Willy looked down, breaking eye contact. He rubbed his hands together and took a deep breath. For a moment Joey thought Willy was having a change of heart and considering accompanying him. Then Willy looked up once more.

"Can I tell you something and you not think I'm crazy?" Willy asked.

"I guess you can."

"I came in and went to bed. I get so keyed up and go so hard on game day, I'm exhausted. I can't keep going like you. But I woke up, having this dream, and it was as if something told me to find you."

Joey stood motionless before repositioning and sitting in one of the tall chairs at the table.

"I couldn't even make out the details, but you were in darkness," Willy continued. "It was like, like you were being stalked." Willy shivered. "Please don't go."

"Willy-"

"Please. It's so late. We have meetings tomorrow. Don't you see? You're having a once in a lifetime season."

Willy stood then and walked to the door. He looked back at Joey.

"Why did you come to Vanderbilt?" Willy asked.

"I came to play football. To be the best college football player ever."

"Then why is this so important? Why is she so important that you're going to risk everything to go see her in the middle of the night?"

Joey rolled the idea around, and for the first time he did see Willy's point. The old Joe barged in and tried to reason with Joey's tormented soul.

"You think she won't be here after the season?"

"No, but I might not be. You don't know. You don't know what's going to happen."

"And neither do you," Willy said. "None of us does."

Willy's persuasion was becoming all too common. His reasoning was impeccable.

Joey walked back into the living room and sat heavily on the couch. He said nothing, but now Willy began to smile.

"Order a pizza... mom!" Joey said. He wasn't angry, but he was disappointed. Maybe Willy had a point. He would have to consider the dream some other day. "The least you can do is order a pizza."

"That's my boy," Willy said. "At least you'll smell good for the team meeting tomorrow."

Who would call themselves the Gamecocks? South Carolina that was who. And the ol' ball coach would have them ready for Vandy.

Chapter 14

For Joey there was nothing quite like the feel of a football in his hands. The dimples, the lumpy laces on his fingers, and the sureness of his grip around the pointy end as he put it under his arm and shoulder all gave him the urge to put his head down and run. He relished everything about the game, and for him it was easy to consider that every carry might be his last. The ride would end. The question was when.

Practices for week five were largely normal for the Vandy team, even though every week had become more and more abnormal. But one thing remained the same and that was the grind of games and the toll they took on the players. All but Joey, who seemed to only get stronger. Playing for five weeks in a row had taken a bit of the spring out of every player's step. Bumps and bruises had begun to hang around. Players who had continued to play through injuries were forced to continue nursing those dings week after week. But after the South Carolina game, they would finally have an off week.

On Wednesday Joey and several of his teammates got the chance to watch the Ol' Ball Coach's weekly show, highlights from last week's game where South Carolina dismantled Arkansas and comments for adoring fans from the legendary head man himself. They watched the Gamecocks' All-American defensive end Ed Tinker wreak havoc with an unprecedented six sacks and twelve tackles. "Looks like he's tossin' a feed sack into the back of a pickup," Coach said. Tinker was 6'7", 260 pounds, and could run a 4.5 in the 40, but watching the game film his speed looked more like 4.4. What was worse, he had a mean streak. He tackled like an alligator procuring its lunch, grabbing ball carriers and then launching his body in the air while spinning them to the ground in a twisted heap. He was solely responsible for ending the season for two quarterbacks already this year.

But the unnerving aspect of the program was the coach himself. A former Heisman Trophy winner, Sean Whittaker had become one of the game's premier offensive gurus. Everything he touched turned to gold. He had coached two national champion teams. He was a scratch golfer. He was wealthy beyond belief after making several shrewd investments with his king's ransom salary. It seemed anything he wanted to do he did.

"They've got a boy who can play. That's for sure," he drawled in his characteristic nasal tone. "He can run and make something out of nothin'. We gotta to contain 'im and we gottta to handle 'im when he plays defense. They've got 'im playin' everywhere on the field. I hope he's plenty tired already."

The coach laughed and curled his nose as he always did when he wanted to be pithy.

"I've been around this game a long time. Special things happen when you have a season like he's havin'. He's gotta stay healthy though."

Joey kept looking at the screen even though the other players glanced at him. Whittaker continued on about how Vandy had not been 5-0 since World War II, and the coach quipped that Saturday might be World War III. He was in fine form.

"They've got some other talent too," Whittaker's sidekick said. "Willy Jackson is tall and fast. He poses matchup problems with everyone's defensive backfield."

"He's good," Whittaker said. "I remember him when he was with Memphis and all the mischief he caused. He's trouble, that's for sure."

"Turn this crap off," Willy said as he stormed away. "I can't stand him."

Joey followed Willy out of the room and the field house then into the parking lot.

"Willy," Joey said walking behind him, but Willy continued walking toward the dorm. "Willy!"

Willy turned around, his eyes red, his face carrying the weight of his past. He said nothing.

"It's over. This is new. There's nothing that man can do to you. There's nothing anyone can do to you."

Willy nodded.

He and Joey walked back to the dormitory, a silent trek. Neither wanted to speak everything on their minds, and that was probably good.

They flew to Columbia Friday morning. Kickoff was at noon on Saturday, nationally televised. As the teams warmed up, the fans filed in filling the stadium to capacity. Joey scanned the sidelines looking for Luan and the cheerleaders each chance he got. But instead of spotting her, he saw something altogether more upsetting. Something that made him worry and gave him doubts. Something he never expected to see.

Al stood on the sideline beside none other than the Ol' Ball Coach himself, animated and laughing with not a care in the world. Joey wasn't sure what the association meant. Was Whittaker involved with Al? Had he been involved with Al for all these years? After all, he had won the Heisman, and everything he touched turned to gold. But he was old. Joey thought that somehow after this year ended, he would… and then he stopped. What did happen after it was all over and the cheering stopped and he was forced to be just another student and another NFL hopeful? Al had never mentioned it, at least Joey didn't think he had.

Now his head was spinning, thinking of all the times he had spoken to Al, the conversations rattling through his head like echoes in a dream.

"Joey!"

It was his turn to catch a pass or run a play; he wasn't certain which. He looked again to the side line. Al was still talking to Whittaker, only this time they motioned his way and both laughed at the joke. Joey began to worry, this time for real. If Al could give it, he could take it away.

Joey began the game by kicking the ball through the end zone, and Carolina's quarterback, a junior that would most certainly go into the NFL after this season, took over. He looked older than his years, sporting a beard and deep lines around his eyes. He was a big man who preferred to try and run over defenders than around them. And while he wasn't the best passer, he could certainly get the job done. He often threw on the run, and he had won games in the Gamecocks' last possession nine times already in his career.

He ran the option on the first play, and Joey found himself one on one. The players collided sending the quarterback backward onto his back.

"Nice hit, freshman," he said, tossing the ball to the official. "I'll be all over it before it's over."

Joey wasn't sure what that meant, but two more plays followed before Carolina was forced to punt. They did so out of bounds on Vandy's 36. Time to see what the Gamecock defense was all about.

Vandy surprised Carolina on the first two plays, both passes to their possession receiver Reynolds that picked up 8 and 12 yards. Inside Carolina territory, Vandy threw a quick out to Willy for 15 more. Now they were at least in field goal range and could take the early lead. But on the next play, Joey took a pitch to the left out of the backfield, and the big defensive tackle Ed Tinker came through untouched. Joey never saw him. The defender exploded through him, sending a bolt of pain from Joey's head down to his toes. His world went black for a moment, and when he rose it sounded as though everyone's words were garbled and slowed down. He tapped his helmet and left the game.

"How many fingers am I holding up?"

Joey could see now. His head had cleared on the way to the sideline. He answered four. Where are you? Columbia.

"I'm okay," Joey said.

"We have to make sure," the trainer said. "Rules."

"I had the wind knocked out of me."

Now the game was real. Joey had never been hit like that, and it shook his confidence. Had Ed made some sort of deal with Al too? Joey was full of suspicion. How could he compete if they were all like that?

As Joey waited to return, Couch through an interception. Without Joey in the game, Whittaker would certainly throw deep, probably where Joey would have been. He tried to tell the coaches he could go back into the game, but it was too late. And on the first play, Carolina threw long to a wide open receiver who took the pass to the house.

"I can go back in," Joey told Michaels.

"Stay out one more offensive series," the coach said. "Go back in when we go back on defense."

Vandy went quietly on offense once more, and the second string punter shanked the ball out of bounds on their own 45 as the first quarter ended.

With Joey in the game, Carolina managed only one first down but it put them close enough to kick a field goal for a 10-0 lead. Then they kicked the ball through the end zone for a touchback. Joey went in at tailback once more. Coming out of the huddle he eyed Ed Tinker, menacing from the defensive line and smiling.

"Freshman is back for more," he said. "Come and get it."

Joey took the counter play and juked back right. But the defense, sensing the play would be run away from Ed guessed right. Joey stopped and dodged, then cut inside, but before he could go any further he felt arms engulf him from behind and Tinker's big head driving him into the ground.

Vandy got two first downs but had to punt once more. Joey kicked the ball out of bounds at the two.

Carolina drove the ball down the field, added a field goal, and went to the half leading 13-0.

No one in the Vandy camp was panicking yet, but things didn't look good. Their line was being slaughtered, especially by Tinker. The Carolina quarterback had carried the ball more than anyone and already had more than a hundred yards rushing. Joey had not been able to get into the game in any real way.

Vandy began the second half hitting Willy on slants every play. He caught passes of 9, 13, 8, 10, and 15. Then on the 25, Couch misread coverage, and Carolina got the interception.

The teams slugged it out through the third, and Carolina started to march at their own ten in the fourth. In a slow drive designed to eat up clock and yardage, they began to chip away. The clock ran, and with only five minutes left in the game Carolina had the ball first and goal on the five. Leading by thirteen, the game appeared to be history.

Vandy took their first time out.

"Man coverage outside. Cheat up. Joey, you're up all the way. You are going to penetrate wherever you see an opening and you are going to hit the ball carrier. Make the tackle. Better yet. We need the ball. We can't give them another score."

The crowd came to its feet as Carolina came to the line. The quarterback waved his hands indicating to the fans he wanted them to quiet and proceeded to go under center. Joey cheated up, further still, behind the nose man whom he patted on the right side. The center noticed. The signal was opposite, and as the nose went left, the center went right. Joey hit him and the quarterback was down right there, a two yard loss.

Carolina took their time, now the clock winding below 4:30. This time Joey cheated up and stuttered on the snap. In a blur he went through the line and collided with the quarterback as he tried to hand off. He held on to the ball though. Loss of three; third and goal from the ten. Under 3:45.

On the next play, Joey saw an opening between the right guard and tackle, hurdled the running back coming up to block and slammed into the quarterback. The ball came free and rolled to the seven where Vandy recovered. Vandy had the ball, but the play was being reviewed.

Michaels was elated, and he had a chance to work.

"Joey, you're in the shot gun. You will run every play. Immediately over the ball. Run it again, but then go back. If they beat us, it will be by beating our best player."

"I'll do it, Coach."

Vandy did have the ball, and they came to the line. Tinker dug in growling.

Joey began to call the snap. He looked at Tinker. And for reasons he didn't even know, he decided that would be a good place to run the play. Anger welled inside him. Something he wanted was being taken away, and Joey became a different man. Never had he felt hatred as he did at that moment.

Joey took the snap, studied the line, saw Tinker swim over the lineman, and as he raged into the backfield, Joey turned and ran at him.

"Aaaaaar," Joey screamed. He tucked the ball under his left arm, and as Tinker began to lower his head and extend his long arms, Joey reached out his right hand in one ninja-like movement and first hit Tinker in the throat then, as he did, wrapped his hand around the man's neck and pushed.

Tinker went sprawling backward, as Joey sidestepped another defender and then began his trek toward the other end. He ran around another defender, did a stop-and-go for another, then ran over the top of the safety who had gotten the angle on him from the right. Tinker finally managed to breathe again, and as the team led him from the field it was obvious his night was over.

After the kick and with 3:25 remaining, the score was 13-7.

Vandy tried the onside kick, but Carolina's front line of good hands receivers recovered. They had to run the clock out. One play up the middle. 3:10 remaining. Another play, this time off tackle, no gain, timeout Vandy. 2:55 remaining and now Carolina was out of timeouts. Carolina pitched to the outside, fell on the ball in bounds for no gain, and when they punted out of bounds 1 minute and 55 seconds remained with Vandy possession on their own 15.

One last meeting on the sideline and Michaels wouldn't see Joey again until after the game.

"Joey, you're in the shot gun. You will run the draw the first play. Immediately over the ball. Run it again, but then fade back instead of running. Willy you post. How far can you throw Joey?"

"I can hit him, Coach."

Joey did as he was told, and the first play went for almost twenty yards. He might have gotten more, but as three defenders bore down on him he stepped out of bounds to stop the clock at 1:15. Then the play.

It seemed to Joey that time went in slow motion. It would have been more dramatic if time had been about to expire, but it was a certainty that Carolina would not be able to move the ball on Vandy at this point if they got the ball back. The Commodores had owned the second half. But as he took the snap, then stepped forward, he could see the entire field at once. Every player read him, every player bit, every player moved forward. And Willy streaked by them, made his cut, and put his hand up. Wide open. Joey stepped back and threw. Touchdown. The extra point.

Vandy held and their record was 5-0.

Chapter 15

Joey enjoyed the week off from football games. But the life of a college football player goes on, and school continues. Not considering short practices and morning workouts, the players got to be more like real students for a change. And when your team is 5-0 and suddenly 16th in the nation, life is good.

Classes were interesting as well for Joey. On Monday, Wednesday, and Friday he had freshman composition, a formality for him since he already had a journalism degree in what he had begun to think of as his past life. He took a philosophy class on those days as well simply because it interested him. His last class of that day was business writing, another easy course for him. And in each of those classes, it seemed that every student took a turn staring at him. He was beginning to grow accustomed to it, but if he thought back at all to who he was, where he had come from, and his actual age, the constant scrutiny creeped him out. He wanted to enjoy the attention, but as of now he couldn't. Joey decided that if he could stay this age, if things worked out that way, he would consider himself nineteen once more and go for all it was worth. The thought of staying this age though and the possible ramifications frightened him, and much of the time he wondered how he had let it get this far.

His favorite class each week came on Thursday afternoon, Beginning Creative Writing with Miss Kuykendall. It was the lone class that forced him to work. Every day he wrote in a journal, and the class began to devour a text book by the famed John Gardener, plowing through it with such vigor he was having difficulty comprehending, writing responses to the theories, and discussing it for the first hour of class. They were also writing stories which were a bit more difficult than he imagined they would be, especially as he tried to apply Gardener's principles. The challenging class brought with it something else as well: Miss Kuykendall. Possibly forty, an hourglass figure, intelligent, and a soft yet firm voice that exuded complete mastery of her subject. Joey had to admit he had a crush on Miss Kuykendall.

Therein was the problem. Nineteen- year-old virulent Joey, really fifty year old Joe Daily, his very situation and station in life made him unavailable to the teacher. Being the creative sort, Joey decided to create a character specifically for Miss Kuykendall. He would give that character a story, littered with backstory about how he had become a widower. He would create himself. He would invent Joe Daily. But for now, he would have to admire her from afar.

Friday arrived and most of the football players went home for the weekend. Preparations were already underway for the Missouri game the following week. There would be no Sunday film sessions, and they would each get the chance to go back to their schools and watch high school football. In that setting they were all famous in their own right. Except Joey. He had nowhere to go, no friends at his "old" school, and no one from his life before Vandy that he could visit. Tyler and even Willy had gone home as well. His Friday consisted of alternately writing Miss Kuykendall's story and dreaming of her.

Joey watched some football on TV Saturday, and by that night he was positively out of his mind. He walked to The Club, threw some darts, and enjoyed his celebrity. By eleven even that had grown old, and he turned to leave. Luan stood before him.

"Hello, sailor," she said smiling.

"Hi, Luan. I didn't see you standing there."

"I thought about coming up behind you and putting my arms around that nice chest," she said. "What would you have done?"

"I have no idea," Joey replied. Everything in his radar sounded a warning, and he couldn't figure out exactly why. He should have relished Luan's appearance. He had sought another encounter since the first, and yet something seemed altogether dangerous and wrong. "I'm heading home. It's late, and I'm tired."

"Joey," Luan pouted, her lower lip protruding as she put one paw on Joey's shoulder and stepped even closer. "Why go slouching toward Bethlehem? The night is so young, and so are you."

Now Joey could feel the cool hand of temptation luring him. His warranted reticence cleared.

"Luan, I'll see you when I can," Joey said. He sidestepped her as easily as he did defenders on the football field, easier than he imagined it would be upon deciding to do so. "See ya' around."

Several young men watched him leaving as they eyed Luan, probably wondering how in the world he could walk out on her and wondering how they could capitalize on the opening. Joey looked back once as he exited and saw Luan smiling in his direction. At least she wasn't history. She wasn't finished by any stretch of the imagination.

On Sunday morning Joey donned sweat pants and a t-shirt, stretched in the lobby, and began running around the campus intent on going to the football field for some sprints. His rest had been recuperative, rejuvenating, and he needed to burn some energy. Oh how good it felt to be nineteen and vital.

Of course, he saw Al, on the same bench, waiting it seemed on Joey's arrival.

"The world is abuzz, my dear boy," Al said, seeming positively radiant.

"That it is, Al."

"Do you find it ironic as I do that we, by happenstance, so often meet on Sunday?"

"It is a strange coincidence," Joey said. He placed his foot on the bench beside Al and stretched.

"I sense," Al said, changing the subject, "that there is a certain young lady absolutely smitten by you. She's a beauty too."

Joey knew at once Al was referring to Luan.

"I think the girls are intrigued," Joey said.

"Joey! Intrigued? My goodness, man, they are atwitter. Sex appeal. That's what it is. You'll make a mint in commercials in due time. If you have due time."

"Al, that's something we need to talk about. I-"

"Joey, you have time. It's been only fifty days. What has happened in fifty days pales in comparison to what's in store for you. I'd dare say Vandy as well."

"I may find a girl yet, Al. I'm so much older though."

"Luan is older than you, Joey. She's quite, how should I say it, striking?"

So Al did know her name and much more about her. Joey was even more certain now of their connection.

"If I have to go back, you know, to being Joe Daily again, I may finally go after someone my own age. I even have my eye on someone."

"Joey, when did you meet Michelle?"

Joey's mind raced back at once, and despite his belief that Al could not read his thoughts and regardless of his attempt at hiding the thoughts of he and Michelle's life together, the scene of their early courtship bombarded his brain. Across the grassy courtyard in college. Freshman year. She couldn't take her eyes off him. For the first time in his life, he ignored every misgiving and walked directly to her. She held her books to her chest like a shield but her smile still failed to hide her interest. Those lips. The soft curve of her neck. The way her finger traced along the spiral on her notebook as she listened to him. Her hand as she shook his in introduction. They were nineteen.

"Nineteen."

Long ago, he thought. Long ago in a time when it seemed the end would never arrive. A time when life was young.

"What if Luan turns out to be like her? What if you met another Michelle?"

"I don't know, Al."

"You never know until you try."

"What I'd really like is to have Michelle back again. That's what I'd like, Al."

"Joey," Al began as if suddenly he was in a great hurry. "One hundred days. It's so fast isn't it. You need a bit more time. Immerse yourself. A bit more time might demonstrate what a wonderful life this can be. No?"

"It might at that," Joey said.

"You've done the figuring, certainly," Al said. "A smart lad such as yourself. You've considered this season, I'm sure."

"Maybe I've thought a bit about it." Joey tried to be cagey and realized at once he was probably outmanned.

"In the Bible. You do read the Bible?"

"I've been known to read the Bible," Joey said.

"In the Good Book. So many times the number forty, rears its head. Poor Moses, in his small, slouching manner, bowed down to God literally if not metaphorically, wandered in the desert for forty years. It rained on Noah's parade for forty days and forty nights. Did you know that Jonah preached in Ninevah for forty days? And who could forget our friend, and what a friend we have in Jesus, who spent forty days in the wilderness? How about another forty days?"

Joey wished he had done his homework. When would that place him? What day would it be?

"Time is of the essence," Al said standing and beginning to walk away. "Going once."

"Add forty. The decision on our deal will be final."

Al stopped and his countenance changed at once. His expression, now absolute steel drawn in a tight mask of what might have been anger and contempt, peered into Joey's soul. He took one step back toward Joey and stopped. Then as quickly as it had gone, his smile reappeared.

"At midnight," Al said. "Midnight. We make it official."

Al turned and walked away, whistling an unknown tune once more, and watching creation amid the arrival of fall in the campus trees. Joey watched as Al turned the corner and disappeared. Only then did he allow himself to shiver.

Chapter 16

Their arms grabbed air. No one could stop him, and to Joey it seemed as though Missouri was playing in slow motion. Joey had six touchdowns in the first half. Willy had two. The score was 56-0. Counting his extra-point kicks, Joey had scored 44 points. He had almost three hundred yards rushing already.

Michaels was tempted to let Joey stay in the game. He wasn't sure what the record for yardage or points was, but surely Joey was within reach. But it seemed that this team and his star player had much more to play for. If Michaels got him hurt, Vandy's season was sunk. And now Michaels believed Joey had a shot at the Heisman. What other player played every position? What other player could boast the stats Joey did?

The coach had been around the game a long time. He became a coaching assistant right out of college. Three years later he took a job at Wilkes University as a line coach. Four years later, he went to UT-Chattanooga as their line coach. He stayed there six years, and with a fourteen- year- old son and a twelve- year- old daughter, he felt the need to be with his family more. He decided to take a job as the head coach at a private school in Nashville. If his dream of becoming a head coach in college was to be realized, it wouldn't hurt to get some real life experience doing just that, even if it was on a small stage.

His high school team did well in their first season, finishing runner-up in the state. But, that spring his son was killed in a car accident. In his mind he had come to Nashville to let his son die.

He had to get away, so he took a job as special teams coach for the Miami Dolphins. Michaels worked hard enough and did well enough to advance to offensive coordinator for Miami as soon as the job sprang open. Then when Vandy came calling, he took the chance and jumped into the shark tank to coach in the SEC.

Michaels knew how suddenly a season can end for a player. Sitting Joey was a no-brainer. He sat Willy as well.

Vanderbilt went to 6-0, and began preparations for Kentucky the following week, the week that the media began to talk about Joey Goodman's chances of winning the Heisman Trophy. His chances of racking up even more impressive numbers and take his team to 7-0 were great.

"The TV people want to film you and Willy," Michaels said. Joey had showered and dressed already after Thursday night's practice. He had stayed busy all week practicing and studying, as well as throwing darts and playing pool at The Club, and he was finally tired. Getting some TV airtime couldn't be all bad though. The prospect was definitely a good PR move.

Joey and Willy dressed in their black uniforms, and by the time they walked to the indoor practice facility the film crew already had cameras, lights, and props sprinkled around a small area in the middle of the field. Every member of the crew looked tired and bored, obviously ready to bag their shots and go wherever they had to go to finish preparing for the game.

Both players were filmed in all sorts of still camera shots, a variety of facial expressions, no expressions, serious pictures, and in one a ball tossed into the air and caught first by Joey and then Willy. The crew moved with precision. The players were almost finished before Joey noticed another conspicuous man gnawing on a pen as he stood along the sideline alone.

Wearing a brown, open button-down collared shirt, khakis, loafers, and chewing the aforementioned pen, it was easy to surmise that the man was a writer. He seemed to be waiting on the shoot to finish, and instead of walking away from him Joey strode in the man's direction when the pictures and filming concluded.

As he approached, Joey mused to himself why the man had been chewing on his pen. He was large, rotund, in a soft sort of way, and it reminded Joey of a younger man named Billy. Billy had been in Joey's dorm many years ago when Joey had begun a fitness kick and started running. Billy told him he believed he didn't believe in running because he thought people only had so many heartbeats in a lifetime and he didn't want to waste his on exercise. Billy countered with the reasoning that since he was running his heart rate was slower and therefore his heart beats were actually fewer. Several years ago, Billy had a heart attack in a bar, staggered to a long table lined with the attendees of a bachelorette party, and fell in its middle sending drinks and assorted salty snacks and candles flying onto the nearby dance floor. One of the girls, thinking a drunk had wiped out their party, whacked him with her purse before she realized he was stone cold dead. He had reached the end of his heart beats. Joey was pondering the man's views on exercise as he neared and spoke to him.

"Joey Goodman?"

"Yes?"

"I'm Nick Bonner," the man said extending his hand which Joey shook. "I'm with *Sports Illustrated*."

The man seemed satisfied with himself and let his place of employment penetrate and reveal its gravitas before continuing.

"Care if I ask you some questions for a story I'm doing?"

"That's fine."

"How did you wind up here at Vandy?"

"Wouldn't you agree that Vandy provides a world-class education?" Joey countered, his senses on high alert and thus his caginess. "I've always loved watching Vandy."

"You know," the man said clearly measuring his words, "I've looked all over for solid evidence of your attendance at McMinn, and even though there is a record of your classwork I can't find a single picture of you anywhere."

"I'm camera shy," Joey said unable to suppress a glance over his shoulder at the recent photo shoot.

"Not a girlfriend one that has a picture of your prom."

"Like I said, I'm shy," Joey said. He smiled.

"I'm doing a story about your meteoric rise to stardom. I had to see you for myself. I can't believe you've never played."

"Remarkable, huh."

"That it is," Bonner said as he scribbled on his pad. "Would you mind if I talk with your parents about their precocious and talented son?"

"That would be difficult. They've passed on."

"I'm sorry. How did it happen?"

"I really don't want to talk about it." Joey was growing restless and concerned about the land mines all around the interview. "Listen, I'm sorry. I'm really tired. It's been a long day."

"That's fine," Bonner said. The man dug into his back pocket and produced a billfold which he flipped open and dug into with a hurried expression of curiosity before finding a business card. "If you find some free time, can you give me a call?"

"Sure," Joey said. He watched the man waddle away and out the door and wondered how many times this scene might play out in the near future. He needed to talk to Al. The thought of doing that swept away his appetite.

Chapter 17

Kentucky was awful. Before the first quarter ended Vandy and all its fans knew the team would go to 7-0. The Commodores could have left Willy and Joey on the bench, and the outcome would have been the same.

Kentucky fumbled the opening kickoff, and Vandy scooped it up and went into the end zone. Then, Vandy picked off a pass on the first play from scrimmage and scored again. Before Joey even touched the ball, the score was 14-0. Of course, Kentucky made the mistake of punting to him after going three and out, and after Joey scored on the play his team led 21-0.

There was an even more curious stat though. Vanderbilt was now starting four walk-ons. Downtown on the offensive line, his brother on the defensive line, and of course Willy and Joey. All four of them were making an impact, the Brown brothers would have been the surprise of the SEC had it not been for Joey and Willy.

The Kentucky final was 70-0.

It would be a lie though to say that because he had Al's help the game was easy for Joey. This was big time college football, and grown men hurled their massive frames into each other like crashing freight trains. The bumps and bruises and even tonight's mild headache confirmed the reality of the collisions for Joey, and even if the score had been lopsided the violence wasn't.

Joey could hear his footfalls in the hall of the quiet dorm as he strode to his room. He opened his door and called "Tyler!", but even his reclusive roommate was nowhere to be found. Strange. The dorm was deserted.

Joey crossed the hall and entered the community room, with its omnipresent, vague aroma of urine and vomit, that lingered in the air no matter how often the room was cleaned. The sad, stained couch sat askew in front of the dark TV.

Joey rolled a yellow number 9 billiard ball on the pool table, bouncing it from the far end back to him close to his own rail. Where was everyone?

"Joey."

He recognized the voice at once, as automatic as breathing, engrained from his first breath. A quickening of pulse, somewhat, a feeling of fullness and safety and love, and yet the expectation of correction or admonishment. Most certainly. That tone meant trouble.

When Joey turned he found not only his mother, but his father, inside the doorway, his father standing with hands on hips, his mother with her arms folded across her chest in her guarded, feminine way. Her head was cocked to the side and slumped over her right shoulder, a look that spoke disappointment as certainly as if she had audibly scolded Joe – for he was Joe now – and a pang of regret gripped his heart as he realized he had somehow disappointed his mother. He did not want to displease his father either, but failing his mother hurt worse. While his father might be angry, his mother was more likely to cry. Joe's transgressions caused his mother physical pain.

"What have you done, Joe?"

This had to be a dream. His parents had been gone more than five years now, dying within a month of each other, his mother of cancer and as far as anyone could tell his father from a broken heart. In his dreams, though, something always appeared to tip the hand of his slumbering mind. This seemed more real, other than the appearance of his long-dead parents.

"Nothing mom," Joe answered. Looking down now, to his hands, he noticed the difference at once. Age spots. Freckles. Below his hands his slightly protruding belly squeezed against his t-shirt. For now, he was no longer Joey.

His mother, in slacks and a collared button-up, brown blouse, looking fashionable even if it was in a last decade sort of manner, turned to look at her husband, deferring a continuation of the questioning as she always did.

"You really think you can beat him? Really?"

Joe was speechless. He didn't know what he thought, like so many other times he had made mistakes his parents uncovered, Joe wasn't quite sure what he planned to do nor why his situation had gotten this far off track in the first place. Why did he do *anything*? Like the time he found the billfold on the side of the road and kept it. He held on to it for several months, thinking he might be able to use the older boy's driver's license, even though he left three dollars inside. He never used the license, but his mother found the wallet while cleaning. There was no difference, and Joe knew he had done wrong and began down that path anyway. Looking at it from his mother and father's perspective, Joey wondered how he could have gone this far.

Then, he thought of Michelle. The pain of guilt was replaced at once by the twisting agony of loss he felt, still, after her death. Then anger, hopelessness, frustration.

"Dad, Michelle," was all he could say in response and grief engulfed him, wrenching his face from the emotion.

His parents, as if by magic, appeared beside him, his father's sandpaper chin against Joey forehead and his mother's soft arms and shoulders, bathed in the aroma of soap and perfume, against his other cheek.

"She can't return," Joe's father said. "She would if she could, even though I can't imagine why you might want her to do so."

"She can," Joe said. He began to back away, the tears flowing freely. "She can! You don't understand! She can!"

"I do understand," his father said, almost under his breath and as if he wasn't even arguing. "I do…"

Joe turned his back, wracked in sobs. She could return. He knew it. Al could make it happen, and Joe didn't care how or what had to take place he wanted Michelle.

Spinning to face his parents, Joe's breath caught in his throat. He wanted to scream, yet he couldn't move. He couldn't look away.

Their clothing hung limp, dirty, and ragged. Their skin hung loose and rotten, their cheeks sunken, their hair lifeless and brittle. They wore no expression, even though his mother's head still tilted to the right, albeit now at an almost impossible angle as if it might tumble off and fall away at any moment.

Joe backed away and found himself sprinting down the long hallway that seemed to telescope away from him. His strength returned, his skin cleared, and he was Joey once more, young and vital. Joey found himself at the end of the hall, looking down from the second story window into the side parking lot. The cars sat amid a boiling river of molten rock. The sky lit at once with the flash of lightning and he swayed back and forth as the rumbling and shrieks of millions of lost souls bombarded his senses. Then laugher, the wicked cackling taunts, the cynical howling and hooting of witches from some long forgotten Halloween.

The flash again, so bright this time as if it was right on top of him. What if he were to be struck by lightning? Could Al save him? Of course he could.

Down below the window Joey saw him. The reporter. His flash bulb illuminated the building. Joey's head swam. Joey's field of vision narrowed, growing smaller and darker, like a closing aperture ending a scene in a movie, until everything was black and silent.

Joey opened his eyes. Only later would he consider that the sensation must be what it feels like to die – longing for the heaviness to pull him down into the darkness. The first thing he saw was Willy's face as it peered down into his, upside down, and his friend's lips moving. At first there was only silence, and then as he regained consciousness the sounds reverberated as if he and Willy were in the bottom of a steel barrel.

"Wake up!"

Even after he could hear Willy and understand what was being said, he could not move. He wanted nothing more than to close his eyes once more.

"Wake up! Don't close your eyes. Look at me."

Joey smelled Willy's breath. Cinnamon. Willy's breath always smelled of cinnamon. Joey tried to stand and Willy held him in place.

"Just stay down a second. You don't smell like booze. What happened? Can you tell me?"

"No," Joey said and then reconsidered. "I mean, I, I don't think I want to talk about it."

"Did you pass out? Faint?"

"I think I did. Let me sit up at least."

Willy relented, and Joey sat up and leaned on his right hand.

"There was a," Joey started, and then realized he couldn't find the word. He could see the image in his mind of the reporter from *Sports Illustrated*, but he couldn't remember what to call him. "The guy that talked to me after the pictures. That-"

"The reporter?"

"Yeah. Him. He was outside the window taking pictures of the building."

Willy stood and looked out the window and down to the parking lot. He saw no one.

"If he was there, he's gone now. Can you stand?"

"I think I can. I'm okay. I feel better now."

"Let's get you to your room," Willy said. He put Joey's arm around his shoulder, and they walked down the hall and entered the dorm room. Tyler sat on the couch reading.

"Hey," Tyler said as he stood. "Is he okay? Joey, you all right?" Tyler moved pillows off the couch and guided his roommate to sit.

"I'm okay. I got a little light headed."

"Let me get a wet rag," Tyler said. As he went to fetch it, Willy sat down by Joey.

"You feel sick or anything?" Willy asked.

"I don't know. Maybe. I think I did." Joey thought back to what he had seen and did feel nauseous. How could he tell Willy?

"We need to go see the trainer. You might have a concussion. Do you remember getting hit or anything? You have a headache?"

"I did have a headache," Joey said. He couldn't remember a specific hit that might have brought on a concussion, but he wasn't sure if he would remember a hit that caused one.

"We need to see the trainer."

"Willy, no. I don't want to go to the trainer." Joey thought about what he might tell the trainer, and knew he couldn't possibly begin to explain the conversation he had with his parents. Joey could hear Tyler rummaging through the bathroom closet. "Willy, is it possible to-," Joey began and stopped.

What if Willy was in the same boat he was? What if he had connections with Al? What if Willy was working with some other "person" like Al? Joey wondered if he could trust Willy. If he couldn't trust Willy, he might be sunk anyway. Should he tell him anything?

"Possible to what?"

Joey heard water begin to hiss from the faucet in the bathroom.

"Would it be possible to cheat the devil?" Joey whispered. He glanced around the room.

"Man, you're delirious."

"No, listen to me," Joey said. He held Willy's shoulder and pulled his friend closer to his face. "We have to talk."

"Okay, okay," Willy said.

Tyler returned and gave the wet rag to Willy who pushed Joey back and placed it on his forehead. He stood and faced Tyler.

"I need to talk him into going over to see the trainer. Can you give us a second?"

"Sure. Sure thing, Willy," Tyler said. "You be okay?"

"I'm fine, Tyler. Thanks. Thanks."

Tyler left the room and shut his bedroom door behind him. Willy sat beside Joey and looked into his face without speaking.

"Willy, have you always been this good at sports? Were you always gifted?"

"Man, I don't know. What do you mean?"

"Don't be modest. It's just us here. Were you always the best?"

"I'm not the best now. These guys we play against, they're all good. I'm not even the best on the team." Willy grew quiet and seemed to be considering his talent. He finally looked back to Joey and said, "Yeah, I've always been good. I was always the biggest and fastest. When I was a kid I was always the first one picked for a team. My team always won. We won the state championship in football and basketball my junior and senior year of high school."

Joey had to take a chance and confide somewhat in Willy. He couldn't tell him everything, but he needed to talk.

"Can you cheat the devil?"

"Why are you saying that?" Willy asked. "What are you saying?"

"I don't know, Willy. I mean, I guess, could you trick the devil?"

"Gra-ma always said 'you don't mess around with the devil'. She said you stay away from that stuff, and you don't have to worry."

"I feel like I'm living on borrowed time, Willy. I feel like I'm going to wake up one day and not be able to play anymore. Or else I'll be gone for good."

"We need to get you over to see the trainer."

Joey consented to see the trainer in the morning if he didn't feel any better. He also allowed Willy to sleep on the lounger while he slept on the couch.

Chapter 18

The following morning Joey's headache still sat behind his right eye, but when Willy asked him how he felt he was able to convince him he felt no different than any other day. The nausea had disappeared, but that might have been because the visions that had haunted him the previous night now seemed like nothing more than a realistic and very bad dream.

Willy did not mention the trainer on Monday, and in fact Joey didn't even see his friend until practice. As Joey was tying his shoes, he heard Willy say, "You okay?"

"Yeah, fine. Thanks."

"No problem," Willy said and walked away. He seemed to have forgotten the conversation, having other things on his mind. That was fine with Joey who wanted to put the whole episode behind him. This was Georgia week.

Georgia's season mirrored their last few seasons. The media began the frenzy with a high ranking and even higher expectations since several key players returned from last year's team. Then, the fans, convinced by the hype, took their expectations even higher. This year, the season began with a loss to Clemson. Unexpectedly, the Bulldogs lost another game two weeks later to South Carolina and dropped to 1 and 2. Now, they were on a four game win streak and it seemed possible they might be able to sneak into the SEC Championship game by winning the eastern division. That was the same division as Vandy at 7-0. If Georgia won however, both teams would have one loss in the SEC and Georgia would own the tie breaker.

Practice went well on Monday working on schemes. Tuesday they would hit in pads. Joey, however, would take a hit before he even got out of bed. Someone knocked on his bedroom door, and he answered in his underwear.

"Get dressed and come look out the window." It was Willy.

"Why?"

"Police. Forensic vehicles. They're everywhere."

Joey could see the parade of flashing lights, and a crowd of uniformed personnel stood gathered around a set of bushes near the student center no more than a hundred yards from Joey's window.

"What are they doing?" Joey whispered.

"No idea. They've been down there a while."

"Anyone know anything?" Joey asked.

"Everyone's looking out their dorm windows. Curiosity. No one knows."

By mid-morning though, ESPN began to carry the story. Nick Bonner, the *Sports Illustrated* reporter, was dead.

"What was he doing there?" Joey asked. He and Willy were catching passes from the quarterbacks as practice began.

"Dying."

"I'm serious, Willy. What could he have been doing?"

"You said you saw him the other night."

"So. I thought I did. That was the other night."

"So how long has he been there?" Willy asked. He took a step to his right and caught a pass before flinging it back.

"How would I know?"

"You tell me."

"I can't," Joey said. He didn't know what else to say. Willy looked on him without saying anything in return then turned his attention back to the quarterbacks and caught another pass. "I mean, I don't know anything about the reporter."

"What will you tell them when they start asking around?"

"Them? Who's them? Tell who?"

"The au-tho-ri-ties," Willy said, enunciating the word. "They'll come around asking. They always do. They're going to want to know if you saw anything. There was a dead man in the bushes right across from the dorm. 'Joey, did you know this man? Have you seen him around?' Then you'll say what?"

"I saw him taking pictures as I looked out the window the other night."

"Then 'I fainted', right?"

"I might leave that part out," Joey said. He caught a pass and held the ball. "I don't know anything more."

"Why did you faint then? What caused you to pass out?"

"I don't know, Willy."

But that wasn't the whole truth. He did know. Joey had seen hell out his window that night. Both players caught passes and said nothing for a bit before Joey broke the silence.

"I need for you to believe me. You're my friend, Willy."

"You don't have anything to do with this? I'm just asking. You don't have to tell me. If you tell me you didn't have anything to do with it, I will believe you. If you did have something to do with this, maybe you should tell me your plan to cheat the devil." Willy looked straight into Joey's eyes.

"Willy, I don't know anything about how that man died."

Willy waited only a second and said, "I believe you."

Joey believed him too, and he felt better after talking to Willy, especially since his friend had not pursued the comment about cheating the devil. Joey wanted to forget that part most of all. At least now he had someone on his side. Someone who believed him. Or at least he thought so. But after practice, when Coach Michaels asked him to come into the office and shut the door, having Willy in his corner still didn't prevent Joey's pulse from rising and his palms from sweating.

"Joey, I know you've heard about Bonner."

"We saw the police cars," Joey said.

"The police were here. In fact, they're still here. Seems your name was all over his notes. He had quite an infatuation with you."

"He stopped me after the photo shoot," Joey began. "He started asking personal questions, and I didn't feel comfortable talking with him. You said freshmen didn't talk to reporters."

"Do you feel like talking to the police?" Michaels asked. "I can tell them no, and we can go to the station with the school's attorney."

"Why would we need to do that?"

"If you know anything else, it would be wise to have legal representation. I'm inclined to think you should anyway."

"I don't have anything to hide. I didn't do anything," Joey said. He almost made himself believe it.

Michaels stood and walked from the room. When he returned two men in suits walked in behind him and shut the door. They introduced themselves.

"Nice to meet you. I'm-,"

"We know who you are," the first detective, a large man with a square head and a moustache that made him resemble Tom Selleck, replied and then smiled.

"Vandy fans," said the second man bespectacled and much smaller with slick hair parted on the side. He looked out of place.

"Bonner, the dead reporter, had your name all over his notes. He must have been writing a story."

"He stopped me the other night after a photo shoot," Joey said. "I didn't answer too many questions."

"Well, it looks like he's been camped out over in the bushes," first detective said. "There were cigarette butts all over. He's quite a fan of McDonald's too. You haven't seen him around the dorm?"

Joey felt compelled to level with the two detectives. He waited just long enough for their smiles to disappear, which probably wasn't a good thing.

"I did see him Sunday evening. He was taking pictures of the building when I looked out the window over the parking lot. I think he might have been taking my picture."

That seemed to satisfy the detectives and their manner returned.

"That's the only time you saw him?"

"Yeah. I didn't see him after that. Willy woke me this morning to show me the commotion."

"Not that it matters, but is there anything special he might have been trying to uncover? We have to ask."

This time Joey didn't hesitate even though he knew the honest answer. The man knew that Joey's story didn't add up.

"I don't have anything to hide," Joey said, realizing it was another of the lies he was going to be forced to perpetrate when he agreed to try out his newfound youth.

"Okay, that's all we've got. Coach," the first detective said shaking Michaels' hand, "take care of this guy. Get him lots of carries and let us have a Heisman winner."

"We get the ball in his hands as much as we can," Michaels said smiling.

After the detectives left, Joey collected his things in the now deserted field house and began walking back to the dorm amid the lengthening shadows of late afternoon.

That was when Al stepped around the corner of a building.

"Joey, my fine fellow. How is the Heisman season progressing? We haven't spoken, my lad."

"You startled me, Al. Things are going fine."

"Are you ready to commit finally? Put this lingering shadow, or should I say specter, to rest, so that you can enjoy this championship season?"

"I'll let you know, Al."

Al repositioned himself in front of Joey, and it seemed as if the man grew a few inches to hover over him. His eyes bore down into Joey, and for a split second the irises seemed to glare bright red.

"You mustn't worry about answering questions," Al said. "I told you, it's all taken care of. You say your parents took you to Little League games, then pictures will appear showing you rounding the bases. Your mother and father were fine people, were they not?"

Joey said nothing and tried to hide his growing fear.

"You must know, Joey, I'm much more powerful than you give me credit. Do you believe me?"

"Yes sir, I do," Joey said. He tried to swallow and found his mouth to be dry.

"Good boy. I look after my flock," Al said and laughed. It seemed as though he had made a joke he could no longer contain. After his laughter subsided he continued in an altogether different tone. "No one, I mean NO ONE," Al said clinching his teeth, "will take advantage of you." Al whispered the last part and moved so close to Joey's face that for a moment it seemed the tall man with the pointy, Italian boots might try to kiss him. "I'd kill anyone, anyone who tried to harm you, Joey."

Al smiled, turned, and walked away into the night.

Chapter 19

The quiet of the locker room unnerved Joey, but it was Downtown Kevin Brown that noticed the silence and mentioned it.

"Why is it so quiet?" he asked Joey.

"It's been more and more this way each week," Joey said as he glanced around the room then broke into a wry smile. "It's pressure."

"From what? I mean what are we pressured about?"

"No, you know, we weren't supposed to win and now we're favored every game. It starts to build and players begin to worry they're going to lose instead of trying to win."

Downtown had begun growing a beard, and now he rubbed his hand along his chin turning the revelation over in his mind as if he contemplated how he might change the situation. Willy did not know the meaning of pressure. If the week's events had created a distraction, no one could have proved it by Willy. Dressed for battle and looking trim and fast, he walked up and stood in front of the pair of gridiron philosophers.

"This guy was watching Uga, the bulldog mascot, licking himself on the field one day," Willy started. "Guy says, 'Man, don't you wish you could do that.' His friend says, 'That dog'd bite yooooou."

"Where'd you hear that?" Joey asked as the laughter subsided.

"I dunno," Willy said and shrugged as he sat by his friend.

"You need to remember that one."

Willy looked around for ears. "I saw it on a forum board."

"What are you doing, man? Coach said we can't get caught up in that. I know. I used to read them all the time. You start reading about yourself though, you know, it can't be good."

"I was bored."

Michaels entered and gave his pre-game talk. The prep had transformed throughout the year. No motivation was needed. The team needed only to be focused and prepared to play. Then, Willy stood.

"Can I say something, coach?"

"You may Willy. Less than a minute though. We need to go."

"It'll take less than that," he said. "Guys, seize this moment. Seize every moment we have. In Shakespeare's immortal words - *he which hath no stomach to this fight,*
Let him depart; his passport shall be made,
And crowns for convoy put into his purse;
We would not die in that man's company
That fears his fellowship to die with us.
This day is call'd the feast of Crispian.

He that outlives this day, and comes safe home,
Will stand a tip-toe when this day is nam'd,
And rouse him at the name of Crispian.
He that shall live this day, and see old age,
Will yearly on the vigil feast his neighbours,
And say 'To-morrow is Saint Crispian.'
Then will he strip his sleeve and show his scars,
And say 'These wounds I had on Crispian's day.'
Old men forget; yet all shall be forgot,
But he'll remember, with advantages,
What feats he did that day.

Willy paused and let the words sink in before continuing.

From this day to the ending of the world,
But we in it shall be remembered-
We few, we happy few, we band of brothers;
For he to-day that sheds his blood with me
Shall be my brother.

    At once every man stood and screamed with a primal and guttural yell. The locker room began to empty. Michaels, Willy, and Joey were the last to leave, and they looked at each other's smiles.

    "Willy," Michaels said, "maybe you should have saved that one for a tougher game."

    "I hope you're right, coach."

    Michaels was right. This game was never close.

Joey returned the opening kick for a touchdown. Willy scored twice on screen passes. The score was 35-0 at the half. Nothing could slow the Commodores, for this team now possessed an enchanted spirit. Even though Georgia might well have been the most talented team Vandy had played to this point, the final score was again 70-0.

There were no chance meetings with Al or Luan that weekend. Throughout preparations the next week for the following game with a depleted and reeling Florida team that was the worst for them in decades, life for Joey was like any other star football player but largely uneventful. They would travel to Gainesville on Friday and play the Gators on Saturday. By all indications the path to the championship and to the Heisman was clear.

Chapter 20

"That speech was pretty amazing," Joey said as the team bus rumbled toward the stadium.

"It wasn't really my speech. It was Shakespeare's."

"I mean, coming up with it, reciting it, before the game. The guys look up to you. Out of all the admirable athletes and great students, they look to you. You have a gift."

Willy stared into Joey's eyes and said nothing for a moment.

"I've always looked to you that way," Willy said. "I never thought they might think I was anything special."

"And there you have it," Joey said. Now he looked out the window and away from Willy before looking back and adding, "That's why."

Joey had no way of knowing if Willy understood what he had said. It was true though. Willy had a knack for deflecting attention. Joey had seen on more than one occasion Willy speak to a fellow teammate and in the process change a bad situation to a positive. Humility. That was it. That was Willy.

The bus rolled down the interstate approaching the stadium. Willy had begun humming a tune that Joey couldn't place, but it was pleasing and instead of thinking about this afternoon's game he closed his eyes and listened without realizing that that was what he used to do when Michelle was alive. It never failed when she was bustling around the house doing whatever she was doing she hummed, sometimes stopping long enough to sing the words to the song in an indistinct, melodic blur almost like background music.

"Joey."

Joey opened his eyes to listen to Willy speaking.

"I meant what I said."

Joey's expression must have told Willy he had no idea what he was talking about.

"I mean, you have this wisdom about you."

"I've seen lots of things I wish I hadn't," Joey said. He thought of Michelle once more. "You have too. Someday you'll get married, get a dog and treat it like a child, and then finally you'll have real children running around the house. You've got a great life ahead of you."

"I wish I could be as certain about that as you are."

"You've got more time than I'll ever have. I'm pretty sure of that."

They didn't speak again on the bus ride. In fact, no one spoke much right up until kickoff.

Florida's best defensive lineman went out with a knee injury weeks before the two teams lined up to do battle, but you couldn't tell it in the first quarter. Even Joey's elusiveness failed to produce more than a couple of first downs. Willy didn't have much luck either. The corner assigned the task of covering him cheated up to the line and hit him as soon as the ball was snapped. Somehow he managed to stay on him so close he never got much of a chance to get down field, and when he managed to begin to get open the line was unable to keep the defensive linemen at bay. If the defense didn't sack Vandy's quarterback, they hurried him or chased him around. Nothing was working.

In the second quarter though, Vandy ran a draw, perfectly executed. Florida, thinking pass, left a wide open and gaping hole that Joey ran through. Impossible to corral in the open field, Joey romped 72 yards for the game's first score.

Vandy ran an onside kick and recovered, then on the first play from scrimmage dropped back as if to pass deep. Letting the defense rush in, Vandy's quarterback Couch dumped a screen to Joey who had lots of blockers and went 55 yards for the second score. Bang, bang, bang and Florida was down two scores. That took the fight out of the Gators. The rout was on.

Final 35-0. Vandy was 9-0.

Chapter 21

Sunday team meetings were almost always the same. Some of the players entered dressed in nice clothes, straight from church services and lunch. A few of the players wore sweats after sleeping in and having a late breakfast. The remaining players wore jeans and Vandy Polo shirts, a comfortable change from how they dressed to attend classes. And, at Vanderbilt during most any quiet moment, many players attempted to isolate themselves for a few minutes and sat away from the group to study. Ten minutes here and ten minutes there, in a tiny cubicle with their backs to the team or in a corner with knees drawn to their chest, the moments became a sizable portion of time as players waited for meetings.

Michaels' meeting changed the tone and feel of the team's entire remaining season.

The coach had something on his mind, and even though he began their meeting with bad news, it seemed to Joey that even worse news lurked somewhere in the back of his mind.

"Last night, Lenny and Dale were arrested at a bar. They're legal age to be at a bar. They were intoxicated and were involved in an altercation. They are suspended indefinitely," Michaels said. He was standing still as he spoke, but after taking several steps and collecting his thoughts, he stopped once more and resumed his talk.

"I can't tell you what to do, nor do I want to. You chose to come to Vanderbilt and play for me and I chose to allow it. I care about each of you. But there's something I need to say, and this concerns all of us.

"I'm not old, but it's safe to say I'm no spring chicken. When you look back on your life, you'd be amazed at how fast time goes by. Things that seemed as though they would never happen, appear and pass in the blink of the eye. You realize when you're my age that you don't have to rush things; things come at you fast enough. By your nature, evidenced in your attendance at Vandy, most of you delay gratification. There's more I want to say, men. I'm having difficulty putting it into words." Michaels stopped and seemed to be suppressing great emotion. Finally he continued. "There's something greater than each of us at play here today."

The choice of words caused Joey's pulse to skip a beat. He looked over to Willy who was staring at the floor and may have been lost in thought. Either way, Willy never reacted. The meeting and Michael's rambling made Joey even more certain that something else was going on that the coach was withholding. Maybe that was a good thing, but it didn't make things any easier.

"Guys, we're 9-0. We, the Vanderbilt Commodores, are nine-and-freakin'-ohhhhh!" Michaels said. He was smiling now, but his expression said something good was happening but something bad was coming along behind this event, as if he couldn't even enjoy his happiness. "You have a chance to do something that few players and teams have ever done. You have a chance to do something that NO Vanderbilt team has ever done. EVER. Do you understand me?"

Heads nodded around the room, and Joey noticed that even Willy was looking up now. He had no expression though. He might as well have been playing poker.

"Three weeks, twenty days from now, our regular season will be complete. Seven more days after that and we'll be in the SEC Championship game if we do what we're supposed to do between now and then. At that point we can worry about all the rest. I'm going to ask you to do something for me," Michaels said and resumed his pacing, looking down to the floor. "And for you."

In the moment of silence someone cleared his throat. There was a rustling of clothing as players readjusted themselves.

"I'm going to ask you to do nothing."

Michaels looked into the sea of expectant faces. The players looked at each other as if there might be some code to decipher what the coach was saying.

"That's right, nothing. I'm going to ask you, for twenty-seven days, to go to practice, to go to classes, to study, to eat, to sleep, to go to games, and in addition do nothing else. I'm going to request that you not go to any social gatherings. I'm going to ask you not to go to the movies. Be boring.

"We have the chance to do something special. The two young men who have been suspended were our teammates. But let's be honest. Those guys have not played all year. They are fine young men and good students, but their roles were limited on this team. One player doesn't make a team. We can do without any one person on this team. I don't want to though. Winning would be more difficult. We are a team. All of us have to continue to buy into the grand scheme if we want to succeed on a broader scale than anyone thinks possible."

"Coach?"

It was Willy, standing now and looking across the room, his brow pulled tight on his high-held head, his countenance angelic.

"Willy?"

"I'm speaking for all of us. We're in." Willy looked around the room at the sea of nodding faces. "I want this more than anything I've ever wanted in my life."

Willy stepped around players in front of him and soon was in a position to address everyone.

"I want to win every game. I'll give a month or two of my life to have something that no one can ever take away from us. I want us all in. If you've got a problem with it, figure it out now. If you don't want to buy in, you need to let everyone know now. I want it all."

Willy looked to Joey.

After satisfying himself that no one had anything else to add Michaels said. "We've looked at the big picture. Let's go small. Do what you're supposed to do every day. Don't worry about two weeks from now. Don't worry about two days from now. Worry about today. And today, we need to talk about the Mississippi State Bulldogs."

Joey looked out among the players, so young and in many ways so naïve. Of all the souls in this room, Joey could empathize more than anyone with Coach Michaels. Michaels was right; the players had lots of time to have fun. Yet, they had only one chance to accomplish what they sought. But how much time did he have? Joey wondered. He had begun to enjoy his youth and his fame and now his scope had narrowed.

Low hanging clouds raced overhead as Joey and Willy trudged back to the dorm. The world had grown cold as if it too waited for the onslaught of a terrible battle.

"They're not good," Joey said.

"It doesn't matter. One game at a time. One day at a time. One moment. Everyone has to make the right decisions for a little while longer."

"Willy, is there more you're not telling me?"

"I want to win. That's all."

"I mean, we're okay, right?"

"Of course. Why would you ask that?"

Joey didn't know. It was an intuition. Just as he had felt as though Michaels had more on his mind, so he did with Willy. It was a gut instinct. They continued walking without speaking until they turned onto the quad where Joey often spotted Al.

As they approached Al's frequent hangout spot, instead of the tall man with his long legs and silver-toed boots pointing off the round, cement bench they spotted Luan. She smiled a quick, curt, melting grin and then said, "Hi boys."

"Hi Luan," Willy said. Joey nodded.

"Can I speak with Joey?"

"Sure," Willy said. He took a deep breath and looked to Joey. "See you later."

So here she was, on cue, as if Joey had been prepped for this moment throughout the afternoon.

"Tell me you have to go study, and I'll scream."

"Don't scream," Joey said, smiling as he looked around the deserted quad. "How ya' been?"

"Joey, I'm good, but I can't understand why you're so scared of me?"

"I'd call it focus, Luan."

"Then let's live a little. All work and no play…"

"Luan, is that what you want?" Joey asked.

"To be truthful, Joey, I want you."

Joey had no response, and when he said nothing Luan stood and hooked one arm in his and pulled him closer.

"It's time to quit being coy," Luan said her face looking directly into Joey's eyes. "I knew it the first time I laid eyes on you. I want you."

"Luan, I'm nowhere close to as naïve as you take me to be. There's no future in us, at least not now. I'm a conquest."

Now Luan was the one who grew quiet. Joey continued.

"Isn't that it? We want something we maybe can't have. The chase is-"

"Stop," she said and put her head into his chest. She might have been crying or it might have been an act, but Joey couldn't tell which. She pulled back a little to look up at him again. "Just stop. You won't even give me a chance. Let me prove it to you. I can fix you."

"Fix me?"

"You have this hole… in your heart… I can feel it. Let me be there, inside you, fix that emptiness, Joey. It's written all over you."

"I can say not now, Luan, and it doesn't mean this thing is over. That's all. I mean not now."

"Boys and their games," Luan puffed. She pulled away and turned around to face away from Joey. "You boys and your games. It's all games. That's all life is, isn't it. This is nothing more than a game to you. I pour out my heart to you and you think this is some game to play with my feelings."

"I don't think I've ever led you on."

Luan turned back to Joey.

"You lead me on by being you."

Luan came back to him and moved dangerously close. Her lower body touched his. Suddenly the afternoon did not seem so cold.

"Take me home," she said and wrapped her arms around him.

"In time," Joey said pushing her away. He wondered for a moment, as he did every time he encountered Luan, how he had the strength and the courage or possibly the stupidity to deny this woman's wishes. "The season ends in January. If we're lucky. Then, let's see where we stand."

"Luck has nothing to do with it."

"In that you are probably correct."

"I won't stop pursuing you," Luan said as if realizing this battle was lost and the war still loomed in front of them.

"I won't stop being interested," Joey said. "I need time."

Luan seemed to consider the comment and then spoke with deliberateness.

"We don't have unlimited time, Joey. You of all people should know that," she said and in the same moment turned to walk away. "Snooze you lose. Don't snooze." She smiled over her shoulder as she strolled away and out of sight.

Joey shivered and walked to the dorm.

Chapter 22

By the time Mississippi State kicked off, Joey was pretty sure he would hear cowbells in his sleep. The noise had become a constant sound hovering around all else like the omnipresent sound of a beehive, the cascade of a waterfall, or traffic on a busy street. Never mind that the bells were against the rules. Their prohibition was never enforced.

Joey collected the end-over-end kick and began his return from the end zone. After nine games, and even though he was operating with Al's help, the game had slowed for him. Joey had always heard about the game slowing down for quarterbacks, and now he understood completely. Accustomed to the speed of the players and able to anticipate movements, Joey had the ability by now to see blocking lanes and walls visibly opening for him. And now, he saw that very thing. To his left, an open avenue where a player had over-pursued to his right. A wall formed behind that where two players blocked in front of a wedge of three defenders. The kicker floundered, slow of foot, behind those groups. This play was a touchdown, and Joey could see it already before it even happened. This play was all over but the celebration. *Ring your cowbell for that* Joey thought.

Then on defense, the same sensation overtook him, as if he could see the play unfold before it even happened. What was more, he could see Downtown's brother Marcus displaying the ability to do the same thing. So, it wasn't only him! Everyone on the team was improving and gaining experience. At the plant, when workers learned how to clean and pack parts they had never done before, Joe often witnessed how they automatically learned shortcuts and what to look for in cleaning, inspecting, and preparing parts for shipment. Now, as Joey, he was doing the same thing on the football field.

On Vandy's first defensive play, Marcus sniffed out a draw and flew into the open hole in the line, collided with the ball carrier, and when the ball popped into the air Joey caught it in stride and flew into the end zone again.

At the end of the day, Joey tallied six touchdowns and the final score was 63-7. Not only was he leading the nation in scoring, but the Vandy defense was now ranked number one as well.

"You were the highlight of the day on Sports Center again," Willy told Joey Sunday morning.

"I get all the credit for our success," Joey said. "The team could do this without me."

"No, that's where you're wrong. They have confidence that you would bail them out if a game comes to that. They don't have to worry."

Joey considered the comment and wondered if it was true. What if he went back to being Joe Daily? Could the team still win? Vanderbilt would face Tennessee next week. The Vols were 9-2 and mathematically still in the hunt for the SEC East title and a berth in the conference championship game. They were a dangerous team that had improved every week. They had confidence. They never feared Vandy nor thought they would lose to the Commodores. The following week, Vandy would play lowly Middle Tennessee State. The real danger would come in the championship game against, most certainly, Alabama, the number one team in the land.

Even though Vandy had risen to number five overall, the Crimson Tide would be double digit favorites, and rightly so. They had no weakness. Even more problematic for Vandy than Bama's talent and history was their coach, possibly the greatest to ever walk a sideline, Nick Sadan. The coach's name in itself had spawned comparisons to the devil himself. The comments arose from jealousy, but his foes had to shake their heads and wonder if some other-worldly power wasn't somehow helping him. Joey believed it to be the case, and he had every right to know it was possible.

Practice for Tennessee week was spirited, and if Vandy needed any help getting mentally focused that bonus came in a

Vols practice report from Wednesday. According to the reports, several of the Volunteer players let it be known that they thought Joey would have difficulty not only doing well against them but escaping from the game unharmed. "If we hurt him, so be it," they reasoned.

Vanderbilt was faced with a conundrum. If they complained to the SEC offices, they ran the risk of appearing afraid of the Vols physical play, thereby giving UT a psychological advantage. If they didn't report it, it might seem like open season to harm Joey.

"We've discussed it," Michaels told Joey. "Do you want us to make a statement and file a grievance knowing full well they will deny it? Or should we handle this in some other fashion?"

"I'm not afraid of them," Joey replied, and that was the truth. This would not be the first game another team had tried to grind him into submission. "We could let it be known that we won't back down. You know, early in the game."

And that was the tactic they decided to use.

Knoxville would be rowdy and loud, but the Vanderbilt players decided that Neyland Stadium would witness a game they would not likely ever forget. Joey thought about Glenn and all the other Tennessee fans at the plastic plant. That was where all this had begun. It was too bad Glenn wouldn't be there to witness their disappointment, especially if everything went according to plan.

Chapter 23

Tennessee's only conference loss on the season came at the hands of the Crimson Tide, and it wasn't pretty. Since then though, the team had regrouped, and now the Vols had begun to think of a rematch with Alabama. They would have to get through Vanderbilt first though, and no other team in the country had a greater margin of victory than the Commodores.

The Vanderbilt team buses, led by Tennessee State Trooper squad cars, rolled down I-40 toward Knoxville passing the blur of evergreens and winter-ready, bare trees on the hills and dales miles away from their destination. Upon arrival the team would eat dinner, go over last minute game planning, and retire to their hotel. The scene had become commonplace for the team, but tomorrow's game was different. For many years, this game had lost its rivalry status due to the one sided nature of the outcomes.

"Willy," Joey said tapping him on the shoulder. "What are you listening to?"

"Call in show."

"What call in show?"

Willy pulled out his ear buds.

"Knoxville. I think it's called 'Vol Calls' or something."

Joey shook his head. Why did Willy refuse to adhere to Coach Michaels' advice and let the fans do the game watching and talking? Willy and Joey had their own worries. But Willy's curiosity got the best of him as well.

"So what are they saying?"

"You really want to know?"

"Sure. That's why you're listening isn't it?"

"I want this edge," Willy said as if he might be considering himself what compelled him to eavesdrop on the thoughts of fans. "I need to know they are out to get us, you know? This one though, this game, I really want to show them. I don't like the *arnj*," he said.

The Volunteer fans might be the most fickle in the nation. When the team was good, they were downright obnoxious. They took ownership of the team during those times, and when they won the Tennessee Valley won. The people became champions. When the team was bad, the fans threw up their hands in sarcasm and looked for scapegoats. Vol football was life itself in East Tennessee. Right now, the team was good, and the fans were rowdy.

"They say they're going to shut you and me down. They say they'll hurt us if they can. They say we'll quit. Want me to go on?"

"I think that's enough." Joey thought about Glenn. He gritted his teeth and looked out the front window of the bus toward the Smoky Mountains.

Over 108,000 fans packed Neyland Stadium, and when the home team ran through the power T it seemed as though the stadium might come crashing down. Joey watched as the Vols ran by. Big. The biggest team they had played yet. His mind wandered to the Bama game. How had they trounced this team the way they had?

Standing in front of the checkerboard end zone, Joey watched the opening kick fly over his head for a touchback. The first, scripted set of downs began. As if expecting the very play that was called, a dive off tackle, UT's big defensive linemen swarmed through the outnumbered right side and dropped Joey for a three yard loss. For the fans the result seemed to be deliverance of a covenant. The second play, a play action pass that should have been a quick hitter in the flat to Willy, got the same result. No one bought the fake, and two men covered Willy. The line swallowed the quarterback couch for another ten yard loss, and he limped back to the huddle in a daze. The noise now was deafening.

"Jesus, what was the third play?" he asked.

"Forget that," Willy said, out of breath. His hands were shaking, and he looked up into the towering levels of seats painted orange. "On second thought."

The clock ticked, but no one said a word. Linemen leaned on their knees. Joey knew where this was going. The play was a quick slant to Willy, unlikely to get the twenty yards needed for a first down. It was as if the defense knew the plays even if Vandy's quarterback suddenly didn't.

"Couch, shotgun, pitch right. Block that way, guys. Willy, slant then cut up as fast as you can run. I'm throwing the ball to the other thirty. You be there when it comes down. No one act like it's not the scripted play."

Vandy went to the line with ten on the play clock. Couch took the snap and pitched right. Joey put his head down and ran for the right sideline with what seemed like the whole Tennessee team in pursuit. After a few steps, he slammed on the breaks and heaved the ball into the air. When it came to earth, Willy was all alone under it and he went into the end zone for the score. The kick made the score 7-0.

"What was that?" Michaels screamed at Couch who didn't seem like he knew what to say. "That wasn't the play."

Willy appeared with Joey by his side.

"Audible," Willy said.

"Audible? There was no audible," Michaels screamed even though he didn't really need to now. The stands had grown quiet.

"Coach, I don't know how, but I think they know the plays."

Michaels turned away and then back to the players at once.

"You run the plays I call," he said. "That's what I get paid for."

Tennessee took the ball and began to march at once with running plays over the tackles. Joey cheated up and made tackles along with the linebackers, but the Vols were eating up chunks of yardage on each try. Vandy's package seemed to focus on the gun-slinging arm of the Tennessee quarterback, but it was evident the Vols planned on using their size to run over and over at the smaller team.

Vandy got a break though, and a bad snap and fumble gave the Commodores the ball inside their own ten. Now they could get some separation with one big play. In the huddle Willy had plans this time. For some unknown reason, his radar had gone off. Something was up.

"Play's pitch right," Couch said.

"Make sure you all go that way," Willy said. "Joey, reverse out of that if they clog things up. I'll cut across and be ready to crack back. The rest is on you. Everybody's going right, you'll go left."

Willy's play worked perfectly. The play did clog up, and when Joey reversed his field all he had to do was outrun three men in containment to the edge. Willy laid the linebacker out, literally knocking him out cold and out of the game. Ninety yards later, Joey gave the referees the ball in the other end zone.

So it went that way throughout the first half. Using Joey and Willy's cunning and speed, Vanderbilt ran busted plays for a total of over 400 yards. The score was 42-0 at the half and the stands were largely empty. Vandy's second team unit played Tennessee even the second half and the final was 49-7.

Only Alabama smokes cigars after defeating Tennessee. Vanderbilt settled for their own locker room celebration now that the team had eleven wins and no losses. They were the Eastern

Division champs and would play in the SEC Championship game. Regardless of the result of that game, unless it was a blowout, it looked like Vanderbilt would be included in the final four-game playoff for the national championship. Next week, they would play lowly Middle Tennessee State. They would most definitely be 12-0. If number one Bama could defeat Auburn, the two teams would meet in Atlanta the following week. Vanderbilt would finally face the man the fans called Satan. What they didn't know was they had probably been dealing with him the whole season already.

Chapter 24

Coach Michaels introduced the new *SI* reporter, a smallish, younger man who looked like the stereotypical fan of every team in the nation, assigned to do the story on Joey. The reporter pushed his thick black glasses into position on his nose and eyed Joey with a star struck gaze and a smile. Joey shook his soft hand.

"Nice to meet you," the reporter said. "Really nice. I'm a big fan."

"That's good. I'm a fan of *SI*."

"I threw away Donner's notes," the little man said as he began rummaging in his bag and producing a camera and a notepad. "To be honest, they were unintelligible. The ramblings of a madman. Maybe he was being affected by his, uh, condition."

Joey nodded in apparent agreement.

"What do you like to do on game day? You know, do you have any rituals or superstitions?"

And that's the way the interview progressed. What was his training routine? Did he think about the moves he made before they happened? Softballs for an hour. Joey was relieved.

Sunday film study and Monday practice was routine. Life was a steady ship, like the calm before a storm. If that was the case, thunder should have rumbled as Joey bounded up the steps to the second floor and his dorm room where upon entering he saw Al leaning back in a recliner, grinning with satisfaction.

"Joey, my lad, how was practice?" Al asked.

"Fine, Al. What have we here?"

Joey's roommate, Tyler, sat in the middle of the couch, almost in what appeared to be a state of shock, like a shy high school boy sitting in the parlor of a brothel. Two lovely, blonde co-eds sat on either side of him, one with her right leg draped over Tyler's right leg and her hand on his small right bicep. His glasses had slid out to the end of his nose.

"These two young ladies wanted to meet the star player, and of course his roommate. Let's hope your trend of being a day late comes to an abrupt end."

"Tyler, you okay?"

"Oh, yeah, I'm fine," Tyler said looking left and then right. "This is Veronica. This is Jessica. I told them I'm a history major."

"I'm sure they like that," Joey said smiling as he tried to reason Al's motives. "Are you staying long, Al? I need to study."

"I'll more than likely leave my guests behind. Had any time to consider what we discussed earlier?"

"Still under advisement, Uncle Al."

"Very well, lad. Very well. You know I'm around when you need to talk." Al stood and walked across the room to the door where he stopped as he grasped the door handle. "The Alabama game is right around the corner."

When Joey said nothing Al continued.

"They're big and fast. Not enough to derail a Heisman contender, but they would seem almost invincible. Don't be upset if that should happen. At any rate, I would imagine the committee would select Vandy to play in the series anyway. I mean, if that were to happen."

"We'll see how we stack up," Joey said, feeling his confidence well up in his chest in a manner he hadn't felt before.

"That you will," Al said. He smiled once more and walked through the door shutting it behind him.

Joey dozed and when he heard the girls giggling and leaving his clock read 2:30.

The next morning it seemed as though life had righted itself once more on the last day of classes before the

Thanksgiving break. That appearance was a mirage. Willy, walking away from the practice field, met Joey who was on the way in. Willy's eyes, red and puffy, told Joey trouble had arrived.

"I'm out for this week's game," Willy said, his eyes downcast as if he was ashamed.

"What?"

"Michaels says they are investigating rumors. Someone brought up the Memphis situation. There's a story coming out. They want to make certain I'm going to even stay on the team."

"That's old history," Joey said. He made a fist with his right hand. "They can't do this."

"They can do anything they want. I'm sorry, man. Maybe this is going to follow me from now on."

"Not if I can help it," Joey said as he strode away from Willy at a faster clip.

"Joey, don't say anything you'll regret. You have a future."

"Not as much as you might think," Joey said. "I won't leave you hanging."

Joey walked through the locker room directly to Michaels' office and walked in without knocking.

"Joey?" Michaels commented looking up from a desk full of papers.

"Why is Willy suspended?"

"The official line is that he's being held out for precautionary reasons. Like during a slight injury."

"Willy is the heart of this team. He hasn't done anything. That old business is just that, old business. He didn't do anything."

"We want this story to disappear, and it will. Maybe not if Willy plays this week. We can win this game without him." Michaels stood and walked from behind his desk to close the door behind Joey. "I believe him, Joey. He's one of, if not the, finest students on this campus and on this team."

"I won't play after this week without Willy."

Michaels sat on the edge of the desk and looked Joey squarely in the eye.

"Do you believe I have Willy's back?"

"I don't know what to believe. I've seen so much in the last few months, I'm having trouble trusting anyone."

Michaels let the comment float out and linger in the cluttered office before continuing.

"I'll take care of him. You may not believe it, but I'm behind you guys, all of you, one hundred percent. You don't need to get worked up about this. You need to tell him everything's okay. Be his friend. Get ready to beat Alabama."

"Honest?"

"Honest."

Joey said nothing else and went to practice. Preparations for Middle Tennessee State wouldn't be the same without Willy, but Michaels was probably right. The Blue Raiders were not in the same league as Vandy this year. In fact, not the same planet. The situation would have to clear by the end of the weekend though. Alabama loomed on the horizon.

The dorm was deserted after practice as everyone made their way home for the holiday. Tyler had departed without Joey fleshing out the situation between his roommate and his new found harem. As Joey pondered over whether Willy had gone home for the holiday himself, Willy poked his head through the door of the room.

"Knock, knock."

"Willy, come in. Are you okay?"

"I'm fine. I talked with Michaels again. I'm good. I get a week off. He told me you stopped by."

"Yeah, I did. I'm not playing without you."

"You're my friend. But you don't have to go that far. I'll be back next week."

They talked about MTSU and even discussed Tyler's new friends. The television was silent. Even Willy didn't want to watch Sports Center. He had no desire to find out if ESPN had caught wind of the true nature of his "injury". He hoped they hadn't. For once, he was following Michaels' advice.

"Are you going home for Thanksgiving?"

"Nah," Joey said, "I'm gonna whip something up here. I don't have anyone to visit, really. It's just me, myself, and I now."

"Then, you're having dinner with me and my grandma," Willy said and before Joey could object he stood and held up his hand. "We'll pick you up at six. We'll go out and have dinner. I'm riding to grandma's house tonight, but we can celebrate Thanksgiving a day early."

Joey struggled to find some way to object, but in his heart that wasn't what he wanted. He wanted to be with Willy and Willy's grandmother.

"She's a bit eccentric, though, so just take what she says with a grain of salt. She's a sweet woman."

Joey asked Willy what he considered eccentric and what he should expect.

"Before she had my mother, she lived in New Orleans. She was a palm reader. It got around the neighborhood in Jackson when I was a kid that she knew black magic. No one would walk by her house at night."

When Willy walked out the door, Joey sat down in the recliner and leaned back to shut his eyes. The holidays had never been his favorite time of year, and after Michelle died that feeling multiplied. The house was always too quiet. The merriment always seemed too merry. There was no more joy in the world, not really. Thanksgiving became a prelude to the misery of Christmas.

Joey tried to summon the strength to dress for his dinner with Willy and Willy's grandmother, and instead watched the shadows from the window grow longer and longer as another of his numbered days lumbered lugubriously past.

Chapter 25

Willy waved from the window of the gurgling Ford pickup which had once been white but now sported more rust than paint. A big busted, old woman who looked no younger than one hundred sat behind the wheel looking straight ahead. Her white hair looked as though it had been styled that very day, and she wore a purple dress with some sort of pin that Joey couldn't quite make out fastened to her right lapel. The thought of the woman driving the truck from Jackson caused Joey to shake his head.

Willy climbed out.

"You sit by Gra-ma? I don't think I can manage my legs around the gear shift."

"Sure." The thought of the woman shifting the gears made Joey smile once more.

"Gra-ma? This is Joey."

The old woman glanced in Joey's direction and nodded once before locking her gaze back on the road once more. Joey entered and slid across the cracking bench seat and decided to sit side saddle toward Willy. The cab smelled of lilacs and emanating from the background another scent reminiscent of a dark voodoo shop in the French Quarter.

Willy closed the door, and Grandma gassed the engine which sputtered only a split second before jolting them out into the open road as Willy cranked the window closed.

"This is Joey I've been telling you about," Willy screamed either over the sound of the truck or to enable the woman to hear him. Joey wasn't sure which.

"You told me his name," the woman spoke in a quiet voice that was not altogether unpleasant or elderly sounding.

"You know where we're going?" Willy asked.

"I know where we're going," she answered before looking over to him and then to Joey. "He thinks I'm senile, and I know more than he does."

Her smile was toothy as she grinned at Joey, melting away any misgivings he might have had. Ginger's Cafe was not exactly what one would imagine for a Thanksgiving dinner, but almost all the other restaurants had closed early for the holiday. The café served vegetables and that was what Grandma Jackson wanted.

The trio entered the restaurant and after ordering sat back and tried to relax in order to break the tension of new people meeting. Instead of asking questions though, Grandma sat studying Joey as the young men made small talk between themselves. She still hadn't spoken by the time the waitress returned with mason jars of sweet tea and took their orders.

"You have an old soul," the woman said finally not breaking her gaze from Joey.

"I think I told you Gra-ma used to have a shop in New Orleans," Willy added looking to each of his companions with an amused expression.

"I guess I do," Joey said. He grew a bit uncomfortable.

The old woman's eyes went to Joey's hands, and a curious expression crossed her face and wrinkled her brow. Her right hand found its way and came to rest on the top of her bust as she breathed in heavily.

"Your hands don't match your body."

Joey's blood went cold, and he tried his best to hide his surprise.

"They're strong and beautiful, but they belong to someone who has seen more than you could possibly know in your limited time on this earth," she continued as she reached across the table and past Willy to Joey's hands.

Her own hands were warm and roughened with deep wrinkles in the palms. Her purple fingernails played along the back of Joey's hands, behind his fingers, before she delicately turned one hand over with its palm up. Then, she performed the same movement on the palm as she had the front along the lines she found there, sending a shiver up Joey's spine.

"Who is Michelle?"

Joey looked to Willy who shrugged his shoulders. Willy had not mentioned any name to his grandmother. Joey thought for a moment and tried to answer, but instead felt a wave of grief and sadness pass through his heart. His eyes clouded. He wanted to tell the old woman everything, to spill his inner most thoughts to her and to convey to her the deep sense of loss and loneliness that had overcome him and lingered in his heart every hour of every day for the last few years.

"She's a girl I used to know," Joey said trying to smile.

The old woman looked up and studied him silently for a few seconds that seemed like minutes. As if the answer satisfied her, she looked down once more.

"She is fine," the woman said nodding as she pursed her lips. "She will always love you, until you meet again."

Now goose bumps raced over Joey's arms and up his neck as if the chill of death itself had passed over him. Joey looked down to his own palm, afraid to raise his eyes for fear that they might give away what remained of his private thoughts. In his palm it seemed as though he could feel the woman's heartbeat from her fingertips, then flashes of light swam in his vision. Joey looked into the woman's face once more, and if he lived a hundred more years he decided he would not want to remember her look of terror and anguish. It passed so quickly that Joey would think back later and wonder if he had seen it at all, and Willy had not been looking, instead gazing at Joey's face. His expression did change as he saw Joey's reaction.

"You're a good man, Joe," the woman spoke in a voice so low now that Joey could barely make out the words. Her hand held his tightly as if Joey might attempt to pull away at any moment. "You did say your name was Joe?"

"Gra-ma, Joey, it's Joey."

"You listen to Grandma Jackson," the woman said ignoring her grandson and focusing her entire attention on Joey. "When the devil is on your tail, you run and hide. You tell the devil to take a hike. Don't need no devil."

"Gra-ma-"

The woman's hand shot up to instantly silence Willy.

"Look into your heart," the old woman said almost rhythmically and as if the words formed the first part of a cherished tune she continued. "Look and see…love never, ever leaves…"

She released Joey's hand and leaned back before taking a deep breath. At some point the food had arrived and now sat around them steaming. The old woman selected a piece of cornbread and picked it from a plate with her gnarly fingers before crumbling it into a bowl of steaming pinto beans.

"Eat your food, boys," grandma said, "it's getting cold. Happy Thanksgiving Joey."

Chapter 26

When they returned to the dorm, Joey and Willy climbed out and Joey said his goodbyes to Willy's peculiar grandmother. He shook Willy's hand as he told him to be careful on the ride, and Willy pulled his friend close and hugged him.

"I told you she was eccentric," Willy whispered.

"Tell her I'll see her again sometime, and we can talk more."

The truck tail lights disappeared around the corner, but instead of walking up the stairs and to his dorm room, Joey strode away from the building and down the street into the night. When he neared the main streets of town he caught a taxi and told the driver where he needed to go. Close to his old house. What better did he have to do?

The evening had grown cold and the wind toyed with the bare tree limbs as Joey turned onto his old street. Most of the houses were dark. A dog barked in the distance. And finally his home, dark as a tomb but otherwise as he had left it, came into view.

As Joey passed he eyed the neighboring homes, Mr. Johnson's place, dark and sinister though in reality it was nothing of the sort even if Mrs. Johnson had been ill, and the Nellums place on the other side, also dark. Joey glanced up and down the street then cut quickly beside Johnson's house and into his own back yard shrouded by trees and some flowering bushes he had planted almost fifteen years ago now.

Joey tried the back door and found it locked. Instead of going to the side door and possibly being discovered, Joey took a few steps and inspected the back window. Sure enough, the screen was still loose. Procrastination sometimes paid off. Six or seven years ago, he locked himself out, and instead of waiting for Michelle to return home, he pried the screen and used a garbage can as a step stool to hoist himself into the window. He fell climbing in though and broke a dish and two glasses. Michelle never let him live it down. He wondered if there were dishes in the way this time.

Joey was much more limber than Joe, and the climb through the window was easier. The exertion served to warm him up as well. Joey hopped off the sink and closed the window behind him. The room was dark in the cold house, and the lack of power had taken with it the popping and "living" sounds that a structure possesses. But with the outside light streaming through the window and his knowledge of the layout of the house, Joey had no trouble navigating through the kitchen and into the dining area. He went around the corner and into the almost pitch black living room area. Somewhere near the mantle there was a flashlight.

Feeling through Michelle's knick knacks she collected brought a wave of something he had yet to experience: the feeling of coming home. He felt the cool steel of the long flashlight and picked it up. But before he turned it on, he sighed deeply in the darkness, breathing in his past and letting the memory soak his soul. A part of him longed to call the whole deal off, here and now. He could pick up the pieces of his life. He could go back to being good old Joe Daily. He could find something to occupy his time.

But what good would it do now? Could he somehow get Michelle back? He knew in his heart what Michelle would say, and he tried to push the thoughts away. He turned on the light.

The couch sat as it had. The rocker looked alone and worn. The television was dark. Joe wondered why he had returned. He had almost succeeded in leaving all this behind and never looking back, but for some odd reason the place had beckoned his return.

Making certain he kept the light low and inconspicuous, Joey ventured down the hall. He glanced into the guest bedroom for no particular reason, didn't need to use his bathroom and passed it by, and then came to his own bedroom. The bed was still unmade. Unlike Michelle, he seldom made the bed unless company might be coming or when he went on one of his rare cleaning sprees.

Maybe it was the sight of the bed or possibly it was the accumulation of the hectic day and week, but suddenly Joey was overcome with fatigue. He considered finding his way back to the dorm, and on second thought decided that he would stay in his house for the night. It was his after all.

Undressing down to his underwear in the cold house, Joey climbed under the covers and pulled them up around his neck. Lying on his back he could almost imagine the various designs that he and Michelle used to imagine forming all manner of creatures and situations as they lay back in the bed during those times when nothing called for them to arise and busy themselves. His imagination played tricks on him as he dreamed he could smell her fading perfume mixed with the light scent of soap that always danced in the night when she climbed into bed beside him.

"I miss you girl," Joey said aloud in the quiet stillness.

As if he could feel her press against him, he rolled away and dreamed that she was behind him, her arm draped over his shoulder, her soft breath in his ear, and then he fell into the deepest slumber he had experienced in months.

Joey awoke to the sound of Mr. Johnson calling his dog, "Heeyah-heeyah, Tippy, heeyah", like a cowpoke out west. In that disoriented moment between sleep and awake, Joey almost thought he was Joe and that nothing had changed. Maybe it was a Saturday and he did not have to rise early, and then he remembered that today was Thanksgiving. Michelle would be… And then, he realized he was awake and things were not the way they were and he was not Joe Daily and Michelle would not be cooking Thanksgiving dinner.

Joey peeked out the window and saw Mr. Johnson standing hands in jacket pockets at the edge of the house, surveying the back yard and the small side yard, then spitting between his teeth. Tippy, his skinny black and white Boston Terrier mix, had returned and was prancing at the man's side trying to gain his attention. Joey dressed and crept out of the bedroom. Though he needed to go badly, he couldn't bring himself to use the bathroom commode. The water would be off. He couldn't do it.

Joey left the back door unlocked as he slipped out and closed it behind him. An indented wall where he usually left a gas can provided enough cover for him to relieve himself behind the house. Then he cut through the Nellums side of the yard and was almost out onto the road when he heard Johnson yell.

"Hey, you, what are you doing?"

"Oh, hello sir."

"I asked you a question. What are you doing?" Johnson asked walking stiffly in Joey's direction. Tippy pranced beside him.

It was time to see what he had learned during his time as Joey Goodman.

"I was having a look at Joe's house. I'm his nephew. Arthur. Nice to meet you."

Joey walked in Johnson's direction extending his hand and smiling. Though he was reluctant, Mr. Johnson took the hand and shook it half-heartedly before sticking his own hand back in his pocket and scolding Tippy to quit jumping on his leg. He must have gathered his wits enough to continue the line of questioning.

"I didn't know Joe had a nephew."

"There's probably lots you didn't know about Joe," Joey said and then wished he hadn't when Johnson's eyes danced hotly.

"What's that supposed to mean?"

"I mean, he was sort of a private person," Joey said. "He didn't go around talking about family and things much."

"I knew Joe better than you might think," Johnson said, looking down to Tippy.

Indeed he did know Joe well. Johnson was the first person Joe had met when they moved in over twenty years ago. Between the two of them they had helped each other bury three dogs, both crying each time, and helped jumped start each other's vehicles more times than they could count. Johnson had sat on the front steps with his arm around Joe late into the night when he lost Michelle, and when Johnson's wife got sick last summer Joe walked the halls of the hospital with his friend until they could bring her home to convalesce where she was most comfortable.

"You talk about him like he's gone," Johnson said.

Joey realized he had been using past tense, but in a sense Joe *was* gone. Joe Daily was in the past.

"I mean, we haven't seen him in a long time," Joey said.

Johnson readjusted his weight moving it from one hip to the other and studied Joey's face. The old man's eyes narrowed.

"You sure you're his kin?"

Joey laughed at the statement and said, "I'm sure. He's talked about you. I don't know why he wouldn't mention me. You have a wife. Margaret. Sweet woman. Likes to can peaches."

"Margaret's dead."

Joey's smile vanished. Looking down now at the top of Mr. Johnson's head, he wanted to wrap his arms around the little man and tell him everything would be fine. He should have been there. Now, everything in Johnson's countenance gave away his sense of loss.

"I'm so sorry, Mr. Johnson."

Johnson looked back up to Joey's eyes that must have revealed something. There was no way Joey could have disguised and hidden his own pain.

"Are you sure we've never met?"

Looking over his shoulder as he began to walk away, Joey replied, "I'm not sure about much of anything anymore."

Instead of catching a taxi this time, Joey walked all the way back to the dorm. The team had an off day, and Joey stretched out on the bed until late that afternoon. Then, he ate a can of beanie-weenies and went to bed.

Chapter 27

Joey stood on the sideline and waited through a television break for MTSU to kickoff. Michaels thought Joey's risk of injury on a special team was higher, so for the MTSU game he would not participate in kicks or punts. Joey scanned the crowd, a sellout of Vanderbilt Stadium, in disbelief. It was the last game of the season, and Vandy was 11-0. What would have happened had Joey not met Al? Willy probably wouldn't have been invited to play as a walk-on. Downtown and his brother would have never played. Including him that was four starters, and he played on both sides of the ball. Joey realized how much time he spent with Willy and began to wonder what things would be like when his time was finished.

"Know what time it is?" Downtown Kevin Brown asked, looming over Joey and looking down with a half-smile.

"What-"

"IT'S GAMETIME!" Downtown screamed picking Joey up and shaking him like a rag doll.

The whistle blew behind them, the kick went through the end zone, and Vandy took over. This week's plan was a vanilla offense and defense. None of that mattered as far as scoring was concerned. Joey got three carries in a row, the third one a thirty yard score. He sat out on defense as Vandy held on three and out. Vandy took over after the punt went out of bounds at the fifty, and Joey scored on a screen pass the next play. His day was finished.

Final 42-0. Vandy had beaten MTSU on the eve of the one-hundredth day since Joe Daily had become Joey Goodman.

"What does it feel like to be undefeated and ranked number two in the country behind Alabama going into the SEC Championship game?" one of the dozens of reporters asked Joey after the game. The ban on freshmen was lifted. It seemed Michaels could trust Joey.

"I'm looking forward to playing Alabama. They're an incredible team," Joey said. "I'm almost afraid to watch the game films."

"How has life changed since you became a Heisman favorite?" another reporter asked.

"Look around you."

"Can you give us a prediction on the game and the Heisman?"

"No way. We're going to do our very best against Alabama. The Heisman is up to you guys. I want to win next week's football game, and I'm going to do everything I can to help our team. If I win the Heisman, they ought to give the award to our team."

Joey was surprised at how easily the answers came, and he wondered if Al's "gift" was helping him in that department as well. He didn't think that was the case but of course he could be wrong.

Joey's creative writing class for the week would be the last of the semester, and it might be the last time he would see Ms. Kuykendall. He was dismayed at his inability to pull off the story he hoped would woo his crush, but the relationship might have been difficult anyway considering how he badly he was still struggling with the loss of Michelle. In the back of his mind a small voice, maybe the echoes and proddings his late wife herself, told him he had to go on with his life. Joey chose to write a fictional and somewhat comedic interview with a "survivor" of the 1980's in the hopes the article would appeal to his professor. Who better to write that story than Joey?

After each of the students read their stories and critiques and suggestions for improvement were offered, the class came to an end much too soon. Joey had difficulty making himself stand and leave the class. He needed to stay behind anyway. He had a gift for Ms. Kuykendall.

"I've really enjoyed the class, Dr. Kuykendall," Joey said as he and his professor walked from the class and into the hallway.

"I've enjoyed reading your work," she said. "I'm not a doctor. I have an MFA in creative writing. Just call me Jamie."

"Good, Jamie. I really have enjoyed the class. You're a professional." Joey fished in his jacket pocket and pulled out tickets to the championship game. "I don't know if the university gives its professors tickets to games or what the situation is, but here are a couple of tickets. I'd love for you to come watch me play."

"Joey, how sweet." She reached out and took the tickets then looked back to him. "You're something. I'd be honored. I'll be there."

Joey nodded and wished he could think of something else to say, but felt awkward and guilty at the same time, almost as if he was doing something wrong. He began to say his goodbyes and walk away when Jamie spoke again.

"If you have an uncle… a brother… a single father… who is anything like you, send them my way. They don't make 'em like you anymore."

"I'll keep that in mind. Maybe I'll see you at the game."

"I hope so." Then she added, "Beat that team. I can't stand 'em."

Everyone in the dorm watched the SEC Championship game special with Willy and Joey. Each time one of their names was mentioned a dozen eyes turned in unison, maybe to see what the player's reaction would be.

The experts were split on who would win, which was surprising in itself to Joey. Alabama was loaded. They had no weaknesses. They had the number one recruiting class each of the last four years. When players left for the NFL, a new batch of stars took their place. The head coach, Nick Sadan, had the best assistance coaches money could buy. The team knew their assignments and so far their game plans had been flawless. They could identify and exploit the weaknesses in each of their opponents.

Game planning began that week, and try as they might the staff had difficulty making the matchup seem like every other game they had played. This game had huge implications. Their opposition was the number one team in the land. Vanderbilt's plan was meticulous, expansive, and serious, all but one instance when one of the coaches could not think of the name of Bama's quarterback.

"The qb," he began. "I can't remember his name. It's an assassin name."

The comment drew a confused look from the defensive unit.

"An 'assassin name'?" one player prodded.

"You know, like James Earl Ray or Lee Harvey Oswald."

"Or John Wilkes Booth?" Joey asked.

"That's it. John Earl Jones!"

Alabama's quarterback might as well have been an assassin. He had a tremendous arm and impeccable touch, like a marksman. Yet, he blended in so nicely, even coaches from the opposing teams failed to remember his name. He had lost only twice in the last three years. And while he might make the trip to New York for the awarding of the Heisman, experts were certain he had no chance to win the award himself. His team, so balanced and so talented, let him remain in the shadows. A silent assassin.

Vanderbilt stayed in the Downtown Hilton. On Friday players met the media. The entire game was a multi-day event that involved fans and built up until kickoff in the Georgia Dome. This game might be round one of a heavyweight fight. Or, it might be the game that eliminated one of the participants. No one knew. And that's where they sat on the eve of the game.

Chapter 28

In their motel room the evening before the championship game, Joey grew bored after finishing his remaining homework. He didn't want to watch the sports channels, knowing that all he would see and hear were constant analysis of the game tomorrow. He had grown weary of watching his and Willy's highlights.

Willy's long frame stretched out the length of the bed with bedside lamp illuminating a book he held on his chest.

"What are you reading?"

"*Run For Your Life* by Tim D. Smith," Willy said. "It's great. It's really sad, but I can't put it down. I keep thinking Josh is going to make it after all. I think he and I are both in love with Tully."

"Well, good," Joey said. He looked around the room and then walked to look out the window down to the parking lot.

"Why don't you kick back a while?"

"I'm bored, Willy. Let's go walk around or something before curfew."

"I'm good," Willy said.

Joey flipped through the flyers on the desk in the room, and among the restaurant coupons he found a calendar. He was studying it when Willy spoke again.

"What did you find?"

"Calendar."

"So what are you doing?"

"Counting days until the championship series," Joey said. He couldn't tell Willy the entire truth, that he was counting the days he had been Joey Goodman.

"You're making me a nervous wreck with all your fidgeting. I can't even read."

"Geesh, Willy," Joey said. "Maybe I'm making myself nervous as well."

If Joey's calculations were correct, and they should have been because he went back and added them up a second time, at midnight on the day of the national championship game his time would be up. A decision would have to have been made at that point. If Vandy didn't make the playoff or if they didn't win the first game of that playoff and get the chance to play for the title, the decision would not affect Vandy.

"I know everyone keeps saying that tomorrow doesn't matter. I mean, if we keep it close it doesn't matter."

Willy looked up from his reading.

"But I don't care, Willy. I want to win."

"We're going to win."

"I am so sick and tired of Vanderbilt always being a team that never wins. We might even have a good season sometimes. Might make a bowl game. I want to win EVERY game."

A soft knocking on the door broke the spell of the conversation causing both of them to look in that direction. Joey raised his eyebrows and initially thought it might be Michaels or one of the coaches.

When he opened the door, Luan stood propped against the framing. She wore a loose, black Vanderbilt long sleeve t-shirt that clung in all the right places and gold, shiny, skin-tight pants. Her right knee was cocked in a way that made her look like she was modeling for a Special K commercial and she appeared to be chewing on a cuticle on her right index finger. Her hair flowed down around her shoulders in luxurious curls, and she smelled wonderful.

"Care if I come in?"

"It's almost curfew," Joey said then thought further. "I suppose a moment wouldn't hurt anything."

Willy was craning his head to see when they walked into sight, and he settled his head back into his pillow and smiled.

"Hi Willy," Luan cooed as she glanced around the room. "Good book?"

"Excellent," Willy said. "What's that perfume?"

"Love Spell," Luan said. "Think it's working?"

Luan smiled and moved beside Joey where she could trace an outline of some hieroglyphic on his right bicep. Joey stepped away, pulled a chair out from the desk, and sat down. His position might make it more difficult to dodge Luan, but it had bought him time and space for now.

"What are you boys up to this evening? The night is still young here in Hotlanta."

"We were just about ready to knock out for the night," Joey said. "Right Willy?"

Luan moved closer to Joey and then plopped down into his lap. Looking to Willy she said, "Sounds interesting."

"Joey, it's not that early. If you want-"

"Willy, you were saying not a moment ago that we needed our rest for tomorrow and we might need to get some shuteye," Joey said as he pushed Luan up and off his lap, almost picking her up into the air in the process. Her hair cascaded out and settled as if she was riding a roller coaster.

Willy finally put the book down and sat up.

"Right, I was," Willy said. He walked over to Luan, took her elbow, and began walking her to the door as her scent wafted along behind her like a lure. "Luan, we'll see you tomorrow. Maybe at the Fan Fare."

Luan walked the last few paces to the door on her own accord, opened it, and looked back over her shoulder past Willy to Joey. She smiled once more.

"I love it when a man plays hard to get. See ya' 'round, *good* man."

When the door closed, Joey walked back into the room and sat on the edge of his bed, smiling and shaking his head.

"She smelled so good."

"I thought you were going to leave me hanging. What were you thinking?"

"I wasn't doing the thinking. She had me under a spell," Willy said. "What is it with you and her? She's been after you for weeks now."

"It's a long story," Joey said, standing and walking nearer to the window to look down into the parking lot. "Maybe I'll tell you sometime."

"Okay. Whatever," Willy said, and at that moment a soft knock sounded once more.

"Oh man, if it's her again, I don't need to let her gain entry. She might attack."

"I'll get it." Willy got up and opened the door.

Instead of Luan, he found Miss Kuykendall standing hesitantly holding a covered dish, as well as her purse and a plastic shopping dangling below.

"Can I help you?" Willy asked.

"Is this Joey Goodman's room? I hope it's not too late."

"It is," Willy said stepping to the side. "Joey, you've got a visitor."

Joey saw who it was and his face lit up.

"Jamie! Hey, come in."

"I made you a little something. I hope you're not on some strict diet or pregame regimen. It's a snack. I wanted to tell you thanks for the tickets and good luck."

"Thank you so much. Really." Joey put the container on the table and turned around to speak to his guest. "So you're staying here in town?"

"Close by," Jamie said. "I brought my sister with me. We'll be cheering as loud as we can tomorrow."

"So are you going back to your hotel? What are your plans?"

"We had dinner. Probably TV and some grading. Just us two old maids."

"Willy, what time is it?"

As if anticipating the question, Willy said, "You have an hour-and-a-half."

"We can go walk around if you'd like. I mean, if you're not doing anything. I've got some time before my coach turns into a pumpkin."

"Sure," Jamie said.

They took the elevator to the lobby where fans were milling around dressed in team colors, either crimson or the black and gold. The crimson fans busied themselves saying "roll tide" to each other, and the Vandy fans tried to ignore them. Joey tried to cover his face somewhat and looked to the ground as they strode out into the cold December evening. Away from the building they found a seat beside a large, lighted fountain that changed colors ever so often.

Joey asked Jamie about her teaching career and then about her own writing. He discovered she was single and that she was thirty-eight. She had a dog named Rowdy who was neurotic. They discussed her aversion to macaroni and cheese. Jamie's sister had been a brat until she was twenty years old. She could still be a drama queen but nowadays fought it bravely.

"You know all about me. Now what about you?"

"There's nothing to know," Joey said. He didn't want to lie to Jamie any more than he already had or that he would have to in order to maintain his secret. It was so wrong in so many ways.

"Do you have a dog?"

"I had a dog named Kevin who loved peanut butter and was a real sweetheart. He died of old age."

"You must have had him your whole life."

Even the simplest instance of unrevised and truthful history was littered with landmines. Kevin came into his life when he was thirty-five. How could he pull this off without lying with every breath?

"I don't like talking about me. I haven't ever done anything worthy of mention until I got to play for Vandy. Sometimes I think I won't ever be able to do anything that permits me to look back with pride."

"You've got plenty of time," Jamie said.

"You never know," Joey said. He looked away from Jamie, possibly in shame but he couldn't be certain.

"Joey, you have an old soul."

"I've heard that before. What does that mean exactly? I mean, what do I do that leads you to believe that?"

"I could see it in your writing. People refer to different things depending on where they're from. It's the same way with writing. A person's perspective is often revealed in the way they refer to items and situations, often depending on their age. You write older than you are."

The conversation drifted away, leaving Joey to struggle for some avenue to continue his nearness to Jamie. Trying to convince her to become involved with him would not only put her in an awful situation but might also be unethical. Joey was pretty sure she wouldn't let things progress that far. So they discussed football and they discussed school. Joey's time continued to fly.

"Einstein was right. Time is relative," Joey said.

Jamie stood. "See? Old soul."

Joey told her goodnight and they parted ways as Joey wondered if he would ever see her again. He made curfew. Then, he tossed and turned in bed all night trying to figure out if Vanderbilt would ever be able to defeat the Crimson Tide.

Chapter 29

At 8:28 p.m. in the Georgia Dome the Alabama kicker pooched a high end over end kick that Vandy fielded on a fair catch at the 33. Vanderbilt tried to run through the line, around the end, and then tried to pass before Joey punted. Alabama ran up the middle twice then ran a screen and was forced to punt.

That was the first half in a nutshell. Try something, try something else, repeat, and then punt. Neither team scored and each trotted to their locker rooms with the hope of figuring out a way to win the game. Both teams realized Alabama was winning the game even though it didn't show on the scoreboard.

The right side of Joey's neck had begun to ache, he thought and oddly enough, from one of the several vicious tackles he had made. Alabama's Heisman contender, a 235 pound running back with over 1,600 yards rushing had dished out as much punishment, if not more, than he had taken. When Joey had the chance to square him up and take him down, the big man had driven so hard Joey could feel it from his head down into his legs.

Vanderbilt decided they would have to somehow get another man in the box, up to the defensive line, to stop the rush. They hoped they could stunt a linebacker on any running down. Surely, Alabama couldn't throw away from Joey all night. The Commodores also decided to commit more double coverage away from Joey and let him operate all alone on receivers.

On the offensive side of the ball, Vandy decided to use Joey in a wildcat formation more often. Joey would take the direct snap and could pass the ball or run it. When he passed, if the defense spread out, he would have more room to run.

Even though Joey hadn't seen Al watching the game, the sight of Sadan roaming the sideline was enough. The coach was as close to battling the devil as any team would ever get the chance.

Joey began to think about the Heisman, not exactly wondering if he was doing enough to win it because that didn't really matter to him, but still contemplating what the broadcasters and voters might be thinking of his performance. Thus far, his play had been solid but not noteworthy. It might be easier if he didn't win. What he wanted was to win the game.

Joey walked behind his teammates as Vandy exited the locker room and walked up the long concourse toward the field, and Joey did spot Al, leaning against the wall and chewing on a toothpick with the light of the field illuminating him from behind and casting a heavenly glow around his head. He was smiling.

"My lad, you're hanging in there. Even better than I thought you could," Al said straightening to his full height.

"They're good," Joey said.

"They are at that. My friend Coach Sadan has them ready," he said then added, "as usual."

"I still haven't decided," Joey told him.

"I think you still have a little time. Not much, but a little. It appears that forty days has come in handy."

"We've got some work to do today if we're going to win the SEC Championship," Joey said. He was the last one in the tunnel.

"I never said I would make a success out of this rag-tag team you play for," Al said. His smile had disappeared, and Joey seemed to be able to see a more sinister side of Al that had become more and more apparent as time had passed.

"I guess not," Joey said. "The outcome is up to us."

"Just don't be too disappointed if the game doesn't turn out the way you hoped. That wasn't part of the deal."

"I won't, Al. Don't you be too disappointed either if we win."

"We'll see, I suppose. We'll see." Al looked out through the gate as the crowd cheered and the teams took the field. "We'll see. I do believe your destiny and your team await," he said motioning with his hand.

Alabama took the opening kick, and as play began they recognized Vandy's tactics and began to dump the ball to receivers away from Joey. The running game was gone, and now they were eating up chunks of yardage with short passes. The first drive culminated with a quick slant for a touchdown, and the Tide led 7-0.

Vanderbilt's first drive was successful as well. Joey, operated out of the shotgun, was able to throw a few passes and also to scramble for two long gains. But when the field grew short, Vanderbilt sputtered and had to settle for a field goal by Joey. The score was 7-3.

Bama's second drive was like the first. This time they scored on a twenty yard fade, away from Joey once more, and the Tide led 14-3.

Vanderbilt's next drive was also like their first. They kicked a field goal again as time expired in the third to make the score 14-6.

Vanderbilt finally held Alabama on the third drive, and when Joey scooped up the bouncing punt and raced to the Bama five it looked as though the Commodores might be able to tie the score with a touchdown and two point conversion. Bama stiffened though and the kick made the score 14-9. Vanderbilt still hadn't tasted the end zone.

And that's the way the score stayed. And stayed. And stayed. Until Vanderbilt took over at their own 18 yard line with four minutes remaining in the game. As if the crowd was no longer in the stands, Joey's concentration came into focus. He hit Willy for a twenty yard gain. Then, he scrambled for 25 more. After an incomplete pass, Joey saw the field open up like the Red Sea, and after he won the footrace to the end zone Vanderbilt was up for the first time 16-14.

Now all Vanderbilt had to do was hold one more time.

"Do your assignment," Michaels told the defense. "You don't have to be a hero. You do your job and if everyone does we'll win this game."

It was easier said than done.

Downtown got blasted all the way to the ground by Alabama's mammoth left tackle, not once but twice. The Tide had abandoned the pass. With two minutes remaining, they planned to get close enough to kick a field goal and they planned to do it on the ground. The big halfback plowed into Joey two times in a row after managing to evade all other defenders, and by the time the clock sat on 21 seconds remaining Bama had the ball on the eight yard line. Third down and six yards to go. Bama had one time out remaining.

The play seemed as though it happened in slow motion. Alabama's big back took the handoff as if he would run over the left side of the line. Instead, it was a counter back to the right. Vandy's front line of defense collapsed, leaving a linebacker in pursuit and Joey who was tied up with a wide receiver. It was clear that the running back would outrun the linebacker, and by the time Joey got free to face him he was in full stride and bearing down like a Mac truck.

Joey bent for the impact and realized that the running back was leaving the ground. As he launched his body, Joey sprung upward, an immense collision that turned the pair in the air and toward the sideline. The running back landed with a thud at the three, and Bama called its last time out with ten seconds on the clock.

"We have to block the kick if we want to win the SEC championship," Michaels said on the sideline. Every defensive player had taken a knee and most of them looked into the coach's eyes.

"We've kept it close," one of the defensive backs whispered. "We'll surely still make the playoff either way.

Like a cat, Willy sprung across the mass of players and came to rest in front of his whispering teammate. For a split second, Joey thought Willy was going to punch the player in the face. Instead, he put a finger not an inch away from his nose.

"We're not losing this game!" he said, gritting his teeth in a snarl. "Not now! We've come too far."

"Willy, let's get our plan together," Michaels said glaring at the whole team.

"I can boost Willy into the air, and he can block it," Joey said.

"Not legal," Michaels countered.

Willy seemed to be thinking, his eyes downcast as if a sweet memory might be crossing his mind.

"Coach, I think I can get it from about where the linebackers stand," Willy said.

Michaels reminded the linemen of their assignments. They had practiced field goal blocks throughout the season, but no one could have predicted how important the play's success might be. As Vanderbilt took the field, their hopes of an undefeated season rode on the most improbable of plays. Alabama had not had a kick blocked in three years. The teams took their positions.

"Willy, the middle?" Joey asked looking to Willy who stood far away where the right cornerback might have stood in a normal defensive set up.

"I used to high jump in high school," Willy said. He was eyeing what looked to be his steps in the run up to the bar. "You try to go in from the right. If you don't get it, I plan to."

The official blew his whistle. The noise in the stadium was deafening. The eyes of the college football were watching.

Bama snapped the ball cleanly and the sound of pads on pads resonated. Joey launched himself from the right side of the Tide's line and he flew past the right-most defender. Yards away he leaped, sprawled straight out like Superman. As he flew, he heard the thud of the kick, and the ball flew through his outstretched hands. He didn't touch it.

End over end, the short kick was and on its way. Willy had begun bounding, then running. Passing a linebacker he tapped his shoulder in a split second as if to say, "I'm behind you." Then, planting his left foot at a forty-five degree angle with his knee straight like a high jumper, he drove his right leg into the air and launched with his back to the line. His right arm stretched, as if he might be reaching for the back of the high jump pad. But instead of reaching out with his hand he turned it straight into the air. Looking over his shoulder, climbing into the air, he could see the ball as it careened toward the field goal. The ball hit the back of Willy's hand near the pinky and ring finger and immediately spun in the opposite direction, sideways now like a helicopter, but still toward the uprights. Wobbling, it veered right. But would it be enough?

In less than a second, the ball hit the lower bar and the right upright with an audible ting, then spun crazy… away from the bar…toward the sideline.. and the horn sounded.

But before the celebration could even begin, the officials began scrambling together. One blew his whistle. Sadan complained from the sidelines, and even though the Commodores had stormed the field the game didn't appear to be finished.

"The previous play is under review," the official announced. "The ruling on the field is a blocked field goal resulting in the end of the game."

"Hey, hey," Joey yelled to one of the referees. "What's going on?"

"The Alabama coach has challenged the block saying the player was aided illegally."

How could it be? In fact, Willy and Joey had considered it but declined when they realized it was illegal. He had not seen Willy tap the shoulder of a teammate, appearing as if he pushed off and into the air. What if the replay gave the appearance that Willy boosted himself up by pushing down on someone's shoulder pad?

Along with the rest of the team, Joey meandered to the sidelines where he saw Coach Michaels who was speaking into his headset. When he finished speaking, Joey stepped in front of him.

"What happens if they rule it was an illegal block?"

"Well, it wasn't," Michaels said, "but if it's a penalty, they're so close they'll assess the yardage, probably half the distance, and they have an untimed down. They'll surely kick again."

What would the chances be of blocking another kick? He had come so close, but Joey didn't think there was any way they would block a second try. What if Alabama went for it?

On the other sideline, Sadan's face was red and he was yelling at the top of his lungs at a poor official that happened to be standing near the yard marker. All the officials had come back onto the field, and when several of them began to dart in the direction of the tunnel, Joey realized that it could only mean one thing.

"The ruling on the field stands. Ballgame," the official said and then ran for the tunnel, underneath a large clock that read 12:10. Midnight had come and gone. The game was over.

Vanderbilt had defeated Alabama 16-14. The Commodores were the SEC Champions.

Chapter 30

The national championship series was set on Sunday as every Vanderbilt player watched together in the meeting room. They weren't watching to see if they would make the small tournament field but rather to see who they would play. First the rankings were announced, and then simultaneously the matchups were released since everyone knew that one would play four and three would play two.

At number four, undefeated Oregon from the Pac-12 coached by Ron Hillerman. The Ducks lead the nation in scoring and have defeated opponents an average of 60 to 12 the announcer said. *The Ducks are led by Heisman candidate Mikey Anitone who has rushed for 18 touchdowns and thrown for thirty more.*

At number three, undefeated Florida State coached by Jimmy Fisherman and highlighted by quarterback and Heisman candidate Brock Leeway. Brock's offense leads the nation in passing with 3,699 yards.

At number two, the Seminole's opponent in the game to be played in Dallas, Texas. The announcer touched the screen and the familiar Alabama logo appeared. *The Alabama Crimson Tide coached by Nicky Sadan and led by Travis Davidson, another Heisman candidate. Davidson has rushed for almost 2,000 yards, and the Tide has lost only once and that to our number one team* he said touching the screen once more *the improbable Vanderbilt Commodores. Vanderbilt will play Oregon in the Orange Bowl in Miami, Florida in their semi-final. Vandy is led by Joey Goodman…*

The rest of the announcement was drowned out by the cheering players and fans that packed the room. Joey's head was spinning. Someone grabbed his shoulders and gave a mighty shake. Michaels had already informed Joey, the overwhelming

Heisman favorite, that they would be flying to New York late in the week for the presentation. Never before had there been such a clear cut choice.

Finals ended on Wednesday for Joey, and for once time dragged by slowly as the weekend trip to New York approached. He strolled throughout the campus, worked out in the weight room – most of the time alone, and tried everything he could think of to occupy his time and his mind. The best thing that happened was the absence of Al, and Luan.

The skyline of New York was even more magnificent than Joey imagined. Although he had lived fifty years, he had never gotten to travel to the greatest city on earth. It seemed as though the skyscrapers went on forever.

Friday was a whirlwind of reporters and meetings. He milled around with all the other candidates and even got to meet many of the former Heisman winners, who not only got the chance to return and revel in their past glory but also voted on the winner themselves. The way they smiled and greeted Joey made it apparent who they had voted for.

"Do you have your speech ready in case you win?" Michaels asked Joey on Saturday afternoon. They were already dressed in suits and ties and they were sitting in the lobby of the opulent hotel.

"I need to look over it once more, but I've got it."

Much of the speech was fiction, and Joey considered thanking Jamie for her help in writing his speech but he thought better of it. He did plan on mentioning his parents, even though they had been gone for several years not recently like most people thought. Joey even considered thanking his "Uncle Al" but could not bring himself to those heights of brazenness and bravado. Many winners would thank God, but Joey shuddered at the very thought of such a statement. Then, he considered the ramifications of his decision should he choose to stay Joey Goodman. No, if he won, and he thought that would indeed be the case, he would make it short and sweet. He would thank his coach and of course his teammates. The sooner he could board the plane and return to plan for the games the better it would be for everyone involved.

Joey sat in the middle of the invited candidates on the front row. He watched each of their highlight reels and was amazed at seeing his own arranged in such a manner. He had reviewed game film all year long, but seeing himself over and over miraculously evading the defense and outrunning would-be tacklers was staggering. Al had done quite a job.

"…it is with great pleasure that we award this year's Heisman trophy to Vanderbilt's Joey Goodman."

Joey shook hands with many of the former winners in a line behind the podium. The applause subsided, and his gaze wandered over the crowd, to his coach and the parents of the losers and all the famous people in attendance. Then he saw Al who sat in the middle of the crowd, smiling with Luan at his side. Their very presence sent a chill down Joey's spine. Why was he here? Was he worried Joey might say something? What would happen if he did?

"I don't deserve this award," Joey began, looking to Al whose happy expression never changed. "My coach and my teammates deserve this award. Teams play football, not individuals. Teams support each other. Teams win together and they lose together. The character of a player is often the reflection of the great character of his team.

"A team can be an assorted collection of individuals that come together for a common goal. A team can be a friend who is willing to sacrifice for the other's success. A team can be a man and a wife who live for one another, sometimes even after death."

Joey paused and looked down at his notes. Even though he thought of Michelle, there was no threat of tears. Still, he dared not look into the crowd and see Al's impish grin.

"At the end of the day, the only thing an individual can do is answer whether or not he has done everything he could do to help his team win. If the answer is yes, that person can smile and with a sigh be satisfied that he has done well. I hope I do the right thing for my team. I hope I can have the courage to sacrifice everything in my life so that my team might live on to fight again."

Joey finished his speech by acknowledging Downtown Athletics, and he began the process of answering a million questions posed by a thousand sports writers.

When Joey and Michaels returned home, a crowd led by his teammates awaited at the airport. They hugged him. They carried him through the terminal. They celebrated with him at the school. Joey kept the trophy overnight and then gave it to Michaels to display at the school. He wondered if he would ever see it again after this season.

"Go home for break," Michaels told the team. "Relax. Meet here at eight a.m. on the 26th. We've got a championship to win."

The team dispersed and Willy met Joey on the sidewalk leading to the dorms. He already had his bag and was pulling it along behind him when he caught up with Joey.

"Are you going home for Christmas?"

"I'll be around," Joey said. "I'm gonna' hang out here until Christmas Eve."

"Go with me. Gra-ma will have more food than we can eat. We'll play video games."

Joey felt in his pocket to make certain he had Willy's gift, but for a moment he didn't pull it out, worrying that Willy might not have gotten him anything and afraid he might put his friend on the spot. Getting a present for Willy was easy; it was the only gift he had to buy.

"If you get lonesome, you call me and I'll come back and get you."

"You know I will. I'll be fine. I've got some reading to do."

Willy opened his bag and pulled out a package.

"Here, I got this for you. Merry Christmas."

Joey took the black and gold box and lifted the lid. Inside was a scrapbook containing press clippings with his picture and headlines cut from a variety of newspapers.

"Willy, how did you do this?"

"Don't thank me. Thank Gra-ma. She put it all together and collected almost all the clippings. It started out for me, but when she found out we were hanging together she did you one too."

"I'm, I'm humbled."

Joey placed the book back inside the box and reached into his pocket.

"I got you this," he said handing the small box to his friend.

Willy unwrapped the paper and pulled out a silver pocket watch which had engraving on the lid.

"We only have so much time to be with true friends," Willy read. "It's beautiful. I'll always cherish this. But we've got lots of time. We're only freshmen. You act like this is the end."

"Go. Have a merry Christmas," Joey said. "I'll see you in a couple of days."

Joey watched his friend walk away and noticed Willy take the watch out of his pocket to check the time as he went.

Joey let himself into the dorm and went to his room. The building was quiet. Too quiet. He wouldn't be able to stand this for very long. He decided to take a chance and go home again and made the long walk across town. By the time he reached the house, night had fallen.

The back door was still unlocked, and he slipped inside, located the big flashlight, and navigated to the living room where he slumped down into his easy chair. It didn't take long to wish he had some heat, but that was something he would have to deal with.

"Merry Christmas, Michelle," he said aloud. The house was silent.

Joey climbed the stairs to his bedroom and began to rummage through Michelle's things. Finally he found what he was looking for.

"Someday, years from now," she had said, "I'll be able to take out all these love notes and make a book. The greatest love story ever. Maybe that's what I'll call it."

The box contained not only love letters, a collection of paper napkins and other bits of white space he had found on the spur of the moment, but also pressed flowers and even a couple of trinkets. Why had she kept all these old things? Did she not know how much he loved her?

On the notes his words returned like listening to echoes, and each letter brought back a tiny memory, some more fully remembered than others but all with a familiar theme. And on the final paper he studied, his windows to his soul absorbed the smooth, elegant sweep of the handwriting and the ideas Michelle left as a ministry to him. Deciding to think more about the particular epistle, he took a deep breath and uncrossed his legs to lean back. How good it felt to uncurl his pliant limbs and feel the stretch of the flexible and nimble muscles. None of that took the place of Michelle though.

"I miss you so much."

Joey heard carolers next door, and he crawled to the window to peer down at Mr. Johnson who stood on the stoop listening. He felt a pang of regret and pity. He might as well have been looking at himself.

Joey made it back to the dorm the next day and even managed to survive until the team returned for practice; it was a nice sight after a brutal holiday. Now things could return to normal, at least Joey's normal nowadays. Would it be sunny and warm in Miami? Joey looked forward to finding out and hoped he could escape the cold and gloom that pervaded Nashville.

Chapter 31

Joey thought Oregon's helmets, and their uniforms, were hideous.

"I like 'em," Downtown Kevin Brown said as the team stretched in unison, lined up in rows like a military unit. "Silver, shiny, with a little slash of green on the side like somethin' from an art museum. The green and gray jerseys. Shiny pants." The big man changed legs along with the rest of his teammates before he looked back to Joey. "Okay, I hate 'em."

"Yeah, now I *really* hate 'em," Joey said.

The Oregon Ducks are too fast for Vanderbilt. Even Joey Goodman. The Ducks defense swarms. Even if Vanderbilt scores, they can never keep up with the west coast style offenses.

Vanderbilt had heard it all week. Even Michaels had gotten in on the act and was now openly encouraging his players to listen. If the Commodore coach wasn't as angry as he seemed, he deserved an Academy Award. He even continued to chirp to his players as he walked along the rows during stretching.

"They think you aren't good enough. They think you don't *belong* here!"

Vandy's detractors looked right early in the game. Oregon kicked off and surprised everyone with an onside kick that one of their men caught on the bounce. Joey stopped him on the seven, but on the first play from scrimmage Oregon beat Vandy to the outside on a sweep and took the lead 7-0. They managed to corral Joey two plays to force a third and one, and when Couch tried to sneak he coughed up the football and one of Oregon's players scooped it up and scored to make the lead 14-0. It looked like the experts were right.

Then, the ship was righted.

Joey returned the kick to the fifty and on first down he slipped through the line and found a crease which he used to outrun the defense for Vandy's first score. Less than five minutes had passed and already 21 points had been scored. It looked like more than a hundred was possible.

But the pace of play changed, and the defenses tightened. Couch hit Willy for a big gainer late in the half, and two plays later Joey capped off the first half scoring with a dive over the pylon and into the end zone. Vandy had figured out how to stop Oregon, and it was only a matter of time until they scored enough to put the game away. Though he didn't say as much, Michaels knew Vanderbilt would win, and his mannerisms spoke volumes to his team.

Vanderbilt scored four more times in the second half, two touchdowns by Willy and two by Joey. Oregon never mounted another serious drive. The Commodores would play for the national championship.

Later that evening in Dallas, Alabama would send a chill through the heart of every Vanderbilt player. The Tide had rebounded from their stunning loss in the SEC Championship game, and they seemed to have blood in their eyes. Florida State never forced a punt. Alabama never had a negative yardage play. Every play they ran worked. Six yards, hand the ball to the official. Eight yards, hand the ball to the official. Ten yard pass, hand the ball to the official. Score, run to the sideline and send in the defense to shut down the 'Noles offense. Repeat.

Final: Alabama 70, Florida State 0.

After the game Sadan was curt. "Now is not the time for celebration. We've got a job to do, and this is the most focused

I've seen us. We'll get down to business tomorrow, and we'll be ready to go to New Orleans and play like we can play."

"Enjoy this win, Co-o-och," the sideline reporter cooed.

"We'll celebrate when the job is finished," Sadan said.

Vanderbilt watched film and did game planning for two days following their win in Miami. To say the mood in Nashville was somber would have been an understatement. And while Downtown tried to lighten everyone's spirits, it was Michaels who finally snapped.

"You guys act like Alabama can't be beaten. We've already beaten them once. If nothing else, that's in their heads. Lighten up and play the game!" he screamed at the end of practice on the third day.

The team flight departed to a raucous send-off two days before the game, and on the flight Joey busied himself with the impossible task of slowing time. He wanted these days to last forever, and it seemed that the only solution to the problem was to complete the deal with Al. Could he force a last minute reprieve of sorts for Michelle? Was it possible? What if he stayed Joey Goodman? Could it be all that bad? Would he not have time to make some sort of penance and offer an apology for salvation anyway?

Landing in New Orleans, these were the very thoughts that played in Joey's mind. If he saw Al again, he would ask him what life would be like should he choose to remain Joey

Goodman. If he could erase the memory of Michelle's letter, tucked in the bottom of his bag.

New Orleans set the tone for the entire championship weekend as soon as the team entered the hotel. A semi-talented jazz band whose members wore funny hats and beads played in the lobby. The team had a short practice and then Michaels, Willy, and Joey spoke at a press conference, again defying the coach's original rule that freshmen could not address the media. At that same meeting of the press, Alabama addressed the media, and listening to them it was difficult to imagine Vandy had won the last game. What was most disconcerting was how angry they appeared.

"Willy, I can't sit around this room all day," Joey said.

Willy was stretched out in bed finishing *Run For Your Life*. He placed his finger where he was in the novel and looked up.

"Josh is running the New York City Marathon," Willy said. "I won't tell you about Tully. I've read all the way to the end, and I'm not going anywhere until I finish. We can walk through the French Quarter if you'll give me another fifteen minutes."

Joey waited, and when Willy put down the book with a heavy, contented sigh they left the hotel, passing Harrah's and venturing into the heart of the French Quarter. Even during daylight hours, the whole place seemed dangerous.

"Willy, I'll show you my boobs if you give me some beads."

"How 'bout you *don't* show me and I give you some beads," Willy said. "Besides, I've seen 'em already, and they're not bead-worthy."

In an open air café, Willy bought Joey what he considered the tastiest dish in New Orleans: Beignets. As they ate the sweet treats, they listened to another jazz band, this one much better. Old couples swayed and danced. Smiles lit up every face in the restaurant.

"You've got powdered sugar on your nose," Willy told Joey. "It looks like you've been partying down here at night."

"Don't let anyone snap a picture. There might be scandal."

"Come on. I want to show you something," Willy said leading Joey out onto the road once more.

They walked up a side alley, past several strip joints and dives, and then turned into another narrow alley before entering through an unmarked doorway. A bell over the door tinkled, and almost instantly a tall, black man wearing a sort of French style hat and shiny purple shirt opened at the collar emerged through a curtain leading to the back.

"Miss Dee here?" Willy asked.

"Can I tell her who calls?" the man said in a higher voice than fit his appearance. His long finger-nailed right hand played with his collar.

"Willy."

The man went back through the curtain and when he stuck his head back through he said to Willy, "Come on back."

They walked through the curtain and down a narrow hallway all the way to the end where the man waved them into the room. Willy's grandmother sat in a wooden rocker, and beside her sat another woman wearing a sun dress with dreadlocks fashioned with multi-colored beads that fell over her shoulders in organized chaos. Both women broke into toothy grins as the young men entered.

"Willy," the other woman said beckoning with open arms for Willy to hug her. "You get taller every time I see you. You look so good."

"Hi, Dee," Willy answered and bent down to give her the requested hug.

"Who's your handsome friend?" she continued, raising her eyebrows and looking first to Willy and then to Willy's grandmother.

"This is Joey. He plays-"

"I know this boy," she cackled. "He been on TV."

She opened her arms for Joey as well, and Joey bent to hug her. She held on to him tightly and squeezed. The woman smelled of incense, and to Joey it seemed as if he was falling into a giant pillow, being pulled down deep into the depths of a feather-bed, time elongating like a dream.

When Joey stood once more, the woman's smile was gone, replaced by a wide-eyed expression that Joey could not place. It might have been surprise or wonder. For a moment she looked almost startled.

"Strong," she said leaning back. "It's easy to see why this one is so famous."

The room seemed to grow quiet at once, and it was as if a chill descended over its occupants. The woman looked to Willy's grandmother who was now serious.

"You knew I would be here, Willy."

"I thought you might, Gra-ma."

"I had to watch my boy. I had to watch this one too. You need as much of the mojo as you can get," she said, turning her head and looking down as though she might have dropped something but yet it was something else altogether, almost as if she tasted something rancid and could not remove the foul morsel from her palate.

Willy suddenly looked like he wanted to leave, to run from the place as fast as he could.

"Wait," his grandmother said perceiving his body language as well as if he had uttered his intentions aloud. Holding up her hand, she motioned to Joey. "Hold her hand."

Joey wasn't sure what he was being told. He hesitated.

"Take her hand," the woman repeated and at the same time extended her own.

At first, Joey felt the hands like one would feel any other person, both leathery and worn, warm and rough. Then, it was as if the light in the room dimmed and a low, persistent hum began to build in the back of his skull through his eyes and nose. Bright colors flashed in his vision, otherwise he could not see. He tried to open his mouth to speak and found himself frozen in place. Then the visions began.

He saw Michelle, in a long, flowing white gown, only she was not old and ravaged with disease. She was not wrinkled and her hair was not turning brittle and white. Instead, she was young, her face tight and smooth and her hair flowing in curled locks over her shoulders and blown by celestial winds. She smiled to him, and put her finger to her lips as if instructing him to be silent even though Joey could not have spoken if he had tried.

Michelle took his hand and pulled him beside her, and as he closed his eyes he felt her engulf his entire body, her familiar smell, her softness, the safety of her embrace spinning him into oblivion. Then, she held him away from her and looked into his eyes, her chin dropping as she studied him to watch his reaction as she always did when she wanted him to really listen.

"Don't..." she said, and the voice echoed like sweet music.

Joey opened his eyes. Tears flowed down the other woman's face, and her cheeks and chin drooped with incredible grief. Gra-ma was serious. Joey released their hands, and Willy nodded releasing them from the old women's spell.

"Hope," Gra-ma said. "Goodbye, boys."

Walking from the building, the tall man with the funny hat nodded seriously in their direction but didn't speak. The door tinkled behind them as they left.

"What just happened in there?" Joey asked as they walked back to the hotel.

"I can imagine, because I've had it happen before," Willy said. "Listen."

Joey turned to look at Willy who was watching each step as he walked along.

"Listen to what?" Joey asked.

Willy smiled. "Just listen. That's all."

Chapter 32

The crowd swelled as Alabama's kicker teed up the ball to begin the game. As Joey turned his back and trotted toward the end zone, he could hear one of his teammates yelling, "So now you wanna' get nasty? We gonna get nasty!"

Two players went down with injuries as the kick sailed through the end zone. This game promised to be what Keith Jackson once called "A Slobberknocker".

When Joey took a pitch on the first play of the game, what he saw looked like a team portrait of the Alabama Crimson

Tide. Why had Couch not audibled out of the play? The second play was a misdirection handoff to the left, and Joey had nowhere to run. Unable to even get started, and even after squirming free from two defenders he was slammed to the ground. Couch had less than a second on the third play before he was swarmed under for a ten yard loss.

No one panicked, yet. Joey punted all the way to the other ten and out of bounds where Alabama took over. The ground invasion began. Davidson left for eight yards. Davidson right for nine. Davidson up the middle for five. The running back looked and sounded like a bull and felt like one as well as they wrestled him to the ground. By the time Bama scored, the game plan was evident. Run the Commodores into the ground until they submitted.

Vandy couldn't physically stop Alabama's defense from running rough shod over the line, but they could outsmart them. On the next drive, Vandy began to dink short, quick hitters over the line. Joey on a screen for ten. Willy on a slant for 12. Then, softening up the rush they slammed through the line, so fast Bama couldn't react. Joey scored from ten yards out to tie the score at 7 apiece. The next two drives were identical, and after one quarter the score was 14-14.

The only reason the score in the first half wasn't higher was due to the fact that both teams were deliberate. Satisfied with four or five yards each play, the offenses ground out drives that lasted minutes each. The score was 28-28 at the half.

Leaving the tunnel for the second half, Joey made certain that he walked beside Willy and Downtown. If he saw Al, he didn't plan on stopping. But what he saw on the field bothered him. High up in the eaves was a clock. It read 10:30. He only had until midnight.

Nothing changed at the half. The two teams had only taken a breather. At the end of three the game was still tied, 42-42. No one had predicted a shootout like this. Then Bama mounted its most methodical drive of the night as the fourth quarter began.

Vandy had committed even more men to stopping the run, but the result was that Alabama was taking three plays each time to get a first down. With nine minutes remaining in the game, Alabama had the ball on the thirty. The real time clock sat at 11:25. At least the game clock was still running. But would Bama grind out a win in the process?

With seven minutes remaining, Bama punched in another score, ironically enough with a short pass this time. The Tide led 49-42.

Vandy began their own drive, and Joey was magnificent even though he was unable to get out of bounds. Now the Commodores were thinking two drives ahead. They had to have enough time to have the last possession. But the drive ended up being slow, and the Commodores got into the end zone with only 4 minutes and 11 seconds remaining.

When Alabama began to eat up clock, it was apparent they planned to get close enough for a field goal as time expired. Three minutes and thirty seconds. Five yard gain. Three minutes and five seconds, six yard gain.

Joey pulled the defense together.

"We have to let them score!"

"What are you saying," Marcus replied, hands on his knees.

"Look at us. We can't stop them. We have to get the ball last."

Before the team could get their wits they were forced to line up once more, and Davidson ran for ten more. The clock continued to run.

"Act like you miss him. Let him score."

The defense nodded to Joey.

Vandy didn't sell the play well, but at least Bama scored. Arm tackles. One player fell on his face. Davidson pranced into the end zone with exactly two minutes remaining.

Vandy fielded the squib kick and had the ball at their own 35 with 1:55 remaining.

Willy came into the huddle and looked to the team. His face was beaming. "Faith. We can do this," he said.

Joey took a handoff for the first play and stepped out of bounds at the fifty after scrambling around. 1:45 remaining. It was 11:45 p.m. Joey ran a draw and was tackled at the forty. First down with the clock running. By the time Vandy got the ball to the ten, only 25 seconds remained. Looking to the big clock in the eaves, he realized he had only eight minutes remaining to be Joey Goodman, unless he somehow made a deal.

Joey ran a sweep down to the three and got pushed out of bounds with ten seconds remaining. Thinking a trick play might get them into the end zone, Vandy called the pitch pass. Running to the right Joey would get the pitch and then look into the end zone. If no one was open he could run for it. They still had one timeout left.

Joey took the pitch and looked to the end zone. Nine, eight, seven, and no one came open. Six, five, four, no one... He fired the ball out of bounds. Three seconds left and time for one more play. It was 11:57.

One last chance, and the play would hinge on Joey's athletic ability. Michaels called a timeout. How could he do that? It was 11:58. The play would never work if Joey Goodman became Joe Daily.

Michaels talked calmly on the sideline, as Joey pranced and tried to cajole his team back to the huddle. The play would take every single Vandy player to the right. Joey would get the direct snap, begin right, and then try to win the footrace to the left corner of the end zone. If they scored, Vandy would go for two. This game would not go into overtime.

At 11:59 Vandy's center snapped the ball back to Joey. In slow motion it seemed, Joey saw his linemen begin to the right. The receiver on the left broke to the back of the end zone, also to his right. The defense followed. Here we go.

Joey slammed on the brakes and pivoted to the left. One man to beat. Sprinting from the ten, he flew. At the five, it looked to be close. He and the defender would arrive at the goal line at the same time. Joey leaped, reached out the ball, and touched the pylon. Touchdown. Vandy was down by a point.

Still the clock sat at 11:59.

"Call the timeout!" Joey screamed.

"We know the play," Couch answered.

Joey had to think quickly. The clock still had not turned to midnight.

"I'm going to be sick! Call timeout!"

Joey ran through the defense, straight for the tunnel and into the darkness as he heard the official's whistle signal a timeout.

And then the strangest thing happened.

The stands grew absolutely silent. Joey could hear his cleats as he came to a stop in the tunnel. With a bright light illuminating his silhouette, Al stood in front of him.

"My lad, I would say that it is midnight. And, it's decision time."

"What will it be like if I give you my signature?" Joey asked out of breath. The stadium sat in still silence and Joey looked back behind him where it seemed that every single person was frozen in place.

"You'll continue to be the greatest college player who has ever lived. My end of the bargain, my boy. At some point, you'll grow old or you'll flame out from your incredible lifestyle should you not be able to handle the wealth and fame. At that point, you'll fulfill the rest of the bargain."

"You can't bring back Michelle," Joey said. He knew it in his heart now. The devil cannot conquer death. That belonged to someone else.

"We don't know that for sure now, do we?"

"I'm afraid we do," Joey said. "I can't do it."

"You mean, you are going to forsake your team. After that oh-so-eloquent speech at the Heisman presentation. After all this, you are going to let Vandy lose again. You may even be forsaking the love of your life."

He paused and waited. Joey looked to the field.

"You really thought you could beat Alabama. My team. My coach, Coach Sadan. I almost let you win."

Joey couldn't believe what he heard.

"You fool!" Al screamed and the stadium rumbled. A terrible groan sounded all around them, and fire lit both ends of the tunnel as smoke boiled in from both ends. Al approached and seemed to swell to ten feet tall.

Then, in an instant, two dark, long and strong arms wrapped around his middle, lifting him from the ground.

Al groaned and shrieked with a primal scream not of this earth as someone lifted him into the air from behind. It was

Willy. Al's body slung from side to side. His head sprouted horns and his face morphed into an elongated and slender visage. He seemed to be screaming to be released, but Willy would not. He held tightly as the pair twisted and writhed in the ramp, smoke swirling around them in the near darkness.

Joey felt it happening. His pads and pants became loose as his muscles left him. His ears began to ring once more. Looking down to his arms, he saw the slender bones return along with his age spots and freckles. He knew he was once again Joe Daily.

"You must bless me," Willy screamed, and as he did Al's body went slack and returned to the form Joey had known. "Be good and I'll let you go."

"Let me go," Al said softly.

Willy released the man, who staggered away, seeming to size up each of them.

"Willy," Al said, smoothing his shirt and pants, "you've already been blessed, and it wasn't by me." Al turned to walk away and stopped to look back at the pair of friends. "You could have had it all, my boy. You could have had it all."

They watched him walk slowly away and disappear at the end of the runway.

"How did you know?" Joe asked.

"I think I knew from the beginning, but Gra-ma helped."

"But how did you do it? How did you…?"

And then he remembered. Willy pulled the watch from his waistband.

"Time," Willy said. "Gra-ma said 'hope'. I told our team 'faith'. The greatest of these is 'love'."

Joe wrapped his weak arms around Willy and began to cry. All was lost. But love had saved him. Once again, the crowd rose to its feet. The noise from the stadium was deafening.

"So what do we do now?"

"We go win the game," Willy said. "You can still run the play. I'll take care of you."

Willy arrived in the huddle first and called the play with Joey behind him. No one saw his face. Joey stood seven yards behind the line in the shotgun. It would be his last play, and Vandy would either win or Al would win.

The ball came back to Joey in a slow spiral and he caught it as he turned to his right. Willy ran from his right flanker spot in a full sprint, and Joey tossed him the ball as he crossed behind. The defense pursued. Joey ran out his fake as if he had the ball and the Alabama team followed Willy. It would be close. Could Willy outrun all of them to the end zone?

Then, as the defense closed in, Willy stopped… and looked right… where Joe Daily limped toward the end zone… all alone. Willy lofted the ball to Joe… who caught it all alone. Vanderbilt won the National Championship.

In a wall of humanity, the Commodores converged on Joe and swallowed him whole. Down he went, and one by one each member piled on top. In the bottom of the pile Joe unsnapped his helmet and began to wiggle out from his shoulder pads, right down to his lucky Vandy jersey. Then, he slipped off his football pants down to his shorts. The only item of clothing remaining was his cleats and he still wore them as he crawled from the pile and walked slowly away from the field. Fans streamed past him to the players, and Joe walked calmly and slowly up the ramp and out of the stadium.

Chapter 33

He saw Johnson out on the stoop as he walked toward the house, and the old man ran as fast as his old body would move out to meet him. They hugged.

"You're okay."

"I'm fine, my friend," Joe said. He pushed the old man away and looked him over. It was a fine sight. "I'm so sorry. I heard about Margaret."

Johnson hugged him once more and cried onto his shoulder.

That evening, as Joe sat in the darkness waiting for his power to be restored, he heard a knock at the door. When he opened it, he saw Willy.

"Can I help you?"

"I think you already have," Willy said smiling. "But yeah, you can."

They walked inside, and Willy looked his friend up and down.

"I need a man, a wise man, to be my manager. Write press releases, look after things. I told you I'd take care of you."

"Now *that* sounds like a good deal," Joe said.

Where is Joey Goodman

When Joey Goodman pitched the ball back to Willy Jackson and then caught the game winning pass in the national championship game, it was the ending to a fairy tale story. But in a fairy tale, the character rides off into the sunset. Joey Goodman didn't just ride off into the sunset. He disappeared altogether. Where is Joey Goodman?

He left his Heisman Trophy. He left millions of dollars in riches on the table. And he vanished. He won't be suiting up any time soon for an NFL team. He won't be playing in the pro bowl. He won't be making inspirational speeches about how the little, unknown guy with unspeakable talent can walk-on and become a superstar on the biggest of all stages.

Or will he?

Will Joey Goodman magically appear once more and take the reins of the football stallion to lead his team to victory once more? Will he tell us where he's been? Or will he leave us with more questions than answers, to try and discover the answer to the Sphinx's question all by ourselves?

Only Joey Goodman knows that answer. And it seems he's not speaking.

Joey, if you're out there reading this, maybe sipping a cup of coffee and remembering the dream we all shared, let me be the first to say "Thank you". You brought a dream to life. You made us believe the impossible is possible. You showed us a once in a lifetime, true and bright, shining star.

Joe, or "Joey" as he once was, set down his cup of coffee. He thought back to the championship season, the year Vandy won the national championship, and he walked off into the Nashville sunset to live out the rest of his life as best he could. And, of course, to be ever mindful of Al lest he ever meet up with him on another dark night.

www.ingramcontent.com/pod-product-compliance
Lightning Source LLC
LaVergne TN
LVHW041614070426
835507LV00008B/235